Stories

from Rhodesia and Zimbabwe
Compiled by Peter Dearlove

FLATDOG BOOKS

Published by Kindle Direct
For FLATDOG Books of Zimbabwe
First published August 2018.
Copyright © 2018 Peter Dearlove
ISBN 9781731481559

Compiled and edited by Peter Dearlove

Peter spent most of his working life in Rhodesia and Zimbabwe, at first as a journalist and magazine editor, and then as the owner and chief copywriter of an advertising agency. In his formative working years he was employed, coached and encouraged by Frank Clements, a prominent Rhodesian freelance journalist and author. Later he went on to work in London for Reuters and Associated Press, and in Hong Kong for The China Mail, before moving back to Zimbabwe and into the world of advertising.
His email address is adwrite72@gmail.com

Dedicated to the memory of Frank Clements, one-time Mayor of Salisbury, free-lance writer, author, and all-round lovely man.

On the left in this rare picture, Frank Clements was photographed with other Rhodesian celebrities at the Pockets Hill studios of RTV during filming of the Mayor's Christmas Cheer Fund Show in 1963. With him were Eric Edwoods (centre), Penny Culverhouse, (right), and Liz Joll, nearest camera.

This photograph was taken in Salisbury prison not long before Rhodesia's Great Escapist, Aiden Diggeden, was due for final release. Because of his frequent jail breaks he spent many more years behind bars than his original sentence demanded, but he settled down and became a model prisoner. It was a friendly moment of mutual respect between adversaries when Inspector Roy Walsh (left) presented Aiden with a signed copy of the Police Outpost publication in which his life story was featured.

Introduction

This slim volume makes no claim to be representative of the literature of the country. None of the 'stories' have been published before, other than the opening chapter which comes from Frederick Selous' wonderful book – *A Hunter's Wanderings in Africa*.

When his book was published, which was less than 150 years ago, there was no country called Rhodesia. The land Selous was wandering around was hardly on the map of western consciousness. To him it was simply part of the great hunting ground called Central Africa. The only passport he needed was the permission of Lobengula, and the occasional co-operation of local tribes. 'Rhodesia' was at least a decade in the future and the slave trade still flourished. Kariba was a narrow gorge he could throw stones across, and there were precious few elephant to hunt.

But it was a place of stories.

In a single chapter Selous conveys to us the plot of at least a dozen – the escape and recapture of two young girls, the Shakunda war, the lawless life of Kanyemba, and the murder of two lovers, being just a few of them.

I hope I do not give the impression that my choice is in any way meant to fill some educational or historical vacancy. The stories are offered here as a form of nostalgic entertainment. I am sure they will only appeal to people who have lived in that wonderful part of the world.

My part in their presentation goes back to my early years as a young journalist when I was working for a man called Frank Clements. He was a freelance writer at the time, but he had also just been elected Mayor of Salisbury. He was not well off, and to survive he had to keep his freelance business going. I was young, cheap, and available, and I was thrilled to get the job. His bread-and-butter contract at the time was a daily morning radio slot sponsored by Matinee cigarettes - *This is Your Land*. It was my job to find promising clips at the National Archives and turn them into 500-word radio scripts. Frank polished my efforts, but I was given a credit line and I thoroughly loved the work. On two other occasions since then I have had the chance to do something similar, and enjoyed doing it enormously. And so when in retirement some colleagues suggested I have a go at this collection I did not need a second nudge.

Putting it all together has mainly been a matter of letter writing – thank heavens for email – and to some extent fact checking. My sincere thanks to all the people who have sent me material, allowed me to edit it, and generally made difficult choices a little easier in getting things rolling. Thanks also to the many others who have helped with checking and proofreading.

The number of stories I was offered was not so great that I could attempt more of a themed collection. The Zambezi River looms quite large, but otherwise the subject matter is vastly varied, and I have therefore not attempted to place the stories in chronological or any other particular sequence. It is intentionally like a Lucky Packet that you can open and dip into anywhere. I hope you enjoy the experience.

In the long process involved in all of this, I came across one photograph that I thought worthwhile including. It is the one of the Great Rhodesian Escape Artist, Aiden Diggeden. I decided to add it as a frontispiece because so many people I spoke to wanted to know what he looked like. Was he even real?

Yes, he was real! Indeed everything you will read in this small collection was real, is real and will be forever real.

The Stories

Once upon a time...

On the Zambezi 1877
Frederick Courteney Selous
From
A Hunter's Wanderings in Africa.

In the morning I went down to look at the mouth of the Sanyati River. The river bed is one mass of huge boulders of rock, and about 150 yards broad; but when I saw it, which was at the end of a remarkably dry season, there was but a mere driblet of water running into the Zambezi. I can easily understand that after heavy rains it may be transformed into a roaring, seething torrent.

The breadth of the Zambezi, where it runs through the narrow gorge of Kariba, in many places cannot be more than sixty yards – narrower than at any other place I had yet seen. It seemed to have worn a deep channel through the hard rock, through which it rushed with a strong current, full of whirlpools and eddies.

To prove the narrowness of the river I threw stones across it in many places, some of which fell a considerable distance on the farther side, though I had to throw without a run, and balancing myself on the tops of rocks.

On November 28, 1877 we crossed the Lusito River and reached Nhaucoe at last. Next day in the afternoon we crossed the Zambezi, and a walk of seven or eight miles brought us opposite a little island, Cassoko, on

2

which resides a Portuguese trader, Senhor Joaquim Mendonza. My Basuto man Franz took the donkeys and followed along the northern bank.

We were now out of the Batongas, the aboriginal inhabitants of the country, and amongst the Shakundas, who are all freed slaves, or runaway slaves, of Portuguese from the countries near the mouth of the Zambezi. The most of them possess flint-lock muskets, and here they owed allegiance to Canyemba, a black man who held some sort of official position under the Portuguese governor of Tete.

Nearly all these fellows had been engaged in the late raid upon the Batongas. Whilst they were away from Nhaucoe, a party of Batongas came round in their rear and attacked the place, burning down almost all the houses; the inhabitants left behind, however, all managed to escape in their canoes across the river. They were now living in little straw make-shifts for huts, on the white sand along the water's edge. There were the remains at Nhaucoe of about eight square houses with verandas round them, the residences of Portuguese traders living here two years ago. There were then, I afterwards learned, over twenty white men here; but they had all left, owing to the badness of trade. Senhor Mendonza alone remained.

A half-breed Portuguese who was living here with the Shakundas came to see us, Gregorio by name. We heard afterwards that a few days before our arrival this gentleman had found out that one of his wives (one of very many) had mistaken another man for himself, and under that impression had committed herself considerably. Mr. Gregorio invited the pair of them to drink beer with him, and, whilst the lovers were enjoying the repast, shot them both dead. No questions were asked about the affair, though the other wives were probably more circumspect in the future.

Upon our arrival opposite the island, Mendonza sent over a boat for us. On the highest portion of the island he had his dwelling- place, a square thatched house, with a wide veranda, in front of which, on a flagstaff, flaunted the Portuguese flag. Besides the large house, there were several store-rooms and outhouses, and below, occupying half the island, a village of Mendonza's slaves and dependants.

Just at sundown two more Portuguese arrived here from Zumbo in a large flat-bottomed boat. One of them was going trading to the Manica country, in company with Canyemba, in a short time; and I afterwards met him there. This man, Mendonza told me later on, had left Portugal at his country's expense; the other, a little man with rather a pleasant face, had belonged to the Zambezi battalion which was sent from Portugal to take part in the Bonga war in 1867. Both of them seemed to be terribly knocked out of time by fever, from which the little man was still suffering.

Mendonza was a tall, spare man, well made, with regular features, dark olive complexion, and fine black eyes. Both now and upon my return from the Manica country he treated me with the greatest kindness, for which I shall ever feel grateful. He was, however, a slave-trader, and treated the natives with great severity. As he expressed it, "Negro diablo, Africa inferno".

November 30

Brought all our goods across from the northern bank of the river to Mendonza's island Cassoko, but left the donkeys in charge of Franz on the northern bank. The first thing that jarred against my prejudices as an Englishman the next morning was the sight of ten Batonga women, just captured in the last raid, all chained together. Each had an iron ring round her neck, and there was about five feet of iron chain between each; some of them were women with little babies on their backs, others young unmarried women. Whilst I was here they were never loosened one from another, but every morning they were sent over in a large canoe to the southern shore, to hoe in a corn-field all day in a row, all chained together. At night they were locked up, still all chained together, in a large, square sort of barn. On the veranda three raw hippo hide sjamboks were hanging, the lower part of each dyed black with blood.

During my stay here another little Portuguese, a fair-haired, light-complexioned man, Manuel Diego by name, also an old soldier from the Zambesi battalion, visited Mendonza. He had with him two very good-looking young Batonga girls (victims of the last raid), one about thirteen or fourteen years of age, the other about ten. He told me he had just bought them from Canyemba.

The morning after he came to Cassoko, he came up in a great rage to Mendonza, telling him the two girls had escaped. I was mightily glad to hear it. It appears that with admirable pluck they had launched one of the large canoes belonging to their master, and, in the absence of the paddles, which were put away every night, had paddled over to the northern bank, a distance of many hundred yards, with their hands. Armed Shakundas were at once sent out to try and recover the fugitives; they were only too successful. On the fourth day, having crossed over to look at my donkeys, I met four Shakundas just embarking for the island with the two poor young girls, who sat in sullen silence, with bent-down heads, and "gyves upon their wrists." My heart bled for them, and had I had the money I would have bought them from Diego. The one cost him a musket, for which he told me he had given £2, and the younger one twenty rupees.

On my return to the island my boys informed me that the two girls had been cruelly beaten, and one of the sjamboks, dyed afresh with crimson stains, told its own tale. It is horrible and unnatural to treat young girls in this manner, and yet this same Diego seemed a mild little man, with a very pleasant, cheerful face.

I have forgotten to mention how the slaves are secured at night after being captured in any considerable number. Large logs are cut by the slaves, from nine inches to a foot in diameter, and in these logs holes are chopped sufficiently large to allow of a man's or woman's foot being put through; other holes are then bored, and wooden pegs driven in, which pass through the holes through which the feet have been pushed, and only just leave room for the ankle, rendering it impossible to withdraw the foot. In this manner five or six slaves are safely fixed up in each log. By day they march with the forked stick round their necks, with which Dr. Livingstone and other travellers have made the British public familiar.

Here, perhaps, a few words concerning the "Basungo Canyemba," as he is termed by the Shakundas. He is a full-blooded black man, and came originally from the Lower Zambesi, somewhere, I believe, in the district of Tete. He speaks Portuguese, and his sons, who have been educated at Tete, both read and write that language. At present he lives on an island in the Zambesi, just at the mouth of the river Kafue, about twelve miles below Mendonza's island. Upon state occasions he comes out in a sort of Portuguese uniform, with a sword. He has a great deal of power in these parts, having a very great number of men all armed with flint-lock muskets, over whom he seemed to exercise the most despotic power.

From what Mendonza told me he seems to be constantly making raids upon any people in the neighbourhood of the Zambezi who have anything to be taken. It was he who, with 600 guns, conducted the late raid upon the Batongas, the effect of which I myself had seen. Sometimes he sends in large parties of his men – two or three hundred – all armed with flint-lock muskets, to hunt elephants.

When he makes an attack upon a tribe, he goes through certain forms. He sends a letter down to the

Governor of Tete, complaining of the injury done to Portuguese trade and Portuguese subjects by a certain tribe, and asking for a *permis de guerra, a* licence to make war upon them, in order to chastise them for their insolence. As far as I could learn, he finds no great difficulty in getting these licences granted. But I am now commencing to relate not what I have seen, but what I have heard, and reports are not by any means to be relied on. Still, he is a man who possesses both the will and the power to do immense harm – a slave-trader and a murderer.

I remained here on the island with Mendonza until the 13th of December. The smallpox was raging among his people and two, three, and four died every day. Owen, not considering it safe to remain, went over and made himself a skerm on the mainland, where Franz, my Basuto lad, was with the donkeys. During this time old Canyemba paid us a visit in full dress, with a large cavalry sword. Mendonza received him with several salutes of musketry, and in an apparently very friendly manner, though he afterwards informed me that he was an awful scoundrel, and calmly added that he was not the friend of Canyemba, but of Canyemba's ivory. I admired his candour and marvelled at his hypocrisy.

A few days afterwards Mendonza and I paid a visit to old Canyemba. He had a large barrack-looking house, and at the back, enclosed within a high palisade, were the residences of the members of his harem, who, to judge from the size of the enclosed space, must have been pretty numerous.

His men had shot two hippo during the night, and the heads had been cut off whole and brought up to the house. At dinner he gave us china plates, knives and forks, and a better-prepared meal than I had tasted for some time. The following morning we returned in canoes to Cassoko, which we reached late in the afternoon after a pleasant voyage up the river, passing many herds of sea-cows on the way.

The mouth of the river Kafue is not very broad – about 150 yards, I think – but it looked very deep, and seemed to pour a very large body of water into the Zambesi.

During my stay at Mendonza's I shot five head of game, all on the southern side of the Zambesi – one zebra, one impala, one wild pig, one black rhinoceros, and one water buck. Owen shot on the north bank one zebra and two water buck.

On the night of December 9 my boys allowed two of the donkeys to stay outside the kraal. The hyenas, which are very numerous and fierce about here, tackled them, and would have killed both had not Owen driven them off with repeated charges of buckshot. As it was, they killed the stallion, and mangled the other badly. I sewed up his wounds next day, and he eventually recovered, only to die of something else. Two nights after this, the boys again left all the three donkeys out. I had been away hunting, and on my return, just at dusk, Franz shouted across the river that the donkeys were away. Mendonza at once called up a headman and a lot of slaves, and, giving them a lantern, told them to cross the river at once and follow the donkeys' spoor, and not to leave it until they found them alive or dead.

In a few minutes we were paddling across the river, but before reaching the shore we heard the hyenas making a tremendous noise, not very far away, and I knew that it was all up with my poor donkeys. We found the spoor, and, following it at length came to the scene of the disaster. The hyenas made themselves scarce, and I had not even the satisfaction of getting a shot at one. We found little more than the skulls of the two sound donkeys, but, strange to say, the one that had been bitten before, and whose wounds I had sewed up, was standing under a bush not far off, and had never been interfered with at all. Slowly and sadly I led him back, cursing hyenas loudly and deeply. The two Batonga men, in whose charge the donkeys had been, had both bolted, nor did they return.

I may myself have unwittingly contributed to the danger my donkeys ran from these ravenous beasts. When the first one was killed, I wished to poison all that remained of him. I had with me two cartridge cases, one containing tartar emetic, and the other crystals of strychnine. When I opened the cartridges the crystals had turned to powder, and for the life of me I could not tell which was the tartar emetic and which the strychnine. As both are disagreeable in their effects I did not care to take a dose to settle the question. So I tossed a coin and set nine baits dosed with the contents of the winning cartridge, which, I think now, must have been the tartar emetic.

All the baits were taken; the emetic no doubt having produced its natural effect, and the hyenas, by severe vomiting, rendered even more ravenous than they were before.

On the Zambezi 1994

An account of a river safari that went badly wrong. From an original manuscript by David Coates Palgrave

A Zambezi river canoe safari is always an extraordinary adventure. There is nothing quite like it available anywhere else in the world. Where the river flows through Zimbabwe and Zambia, some hundreds of miles through uninhabited lands, is where those safaris begin and end, and they pass through a world where people fear to tread. The scenery is spectacular, and for much of the journey the river itself ambles along lazily enough, making for travellers a comfortable ride. But it is nevertheless darkest, wildest Africa there, and any comfort is often accompanied by gut-wrenching apprehension, and sometimes terror. That is the big attraction.

Along that stretch of the river the north bank is in Zambia, the south Zimbabwe. Both sides are wild, and home to large numbers of very fearsome creatures indeed. Hippo and crocodile infest those waters. Lion, elephant, buffalo, hyena, leopard and snakes of various shades and stripe, share the surrounding land. There is little place for humans, none has been set aside for their exclusive use. There are no hotels, hospitals, clinics, or luxuries. Airstrips are few and communications poor. There are no roads to speak of. If you get into difficulties on one of these adventures you can be in serious trouble, mortal danger no less.

There have been many incidents, but none more astonishing than the two that took place one day in April, 1994. I know about them intimately because my brother was at the very heart of the dramatic chain of events that shocked and rocked the lives of many people.

My brother, Phil, had been a canoe safari guide on the Zambezi for two years. Bearded and tanned, with long curly locks bleached by the African sun falling almost to his shoulders; sparkling green eyes fringed by thick dark lashes, he was the image of vitality and health, radiating good humour and an irrepressible sense of fun. Shoeless for the most part, clad always in an old pair of rafting shorts and faded T-shirt, all he owned in the world could be stuffed into his battered rucksack. This barefoot young man of under 20 years old was treasured by his family and friends. His cheeky grin and infectious laugh endeared him to all he met and he was a very popular and knowledgeable guide.

For his first assignment that April Phil had planned an Easter safari gift to his sister Nicky and a couple of friends, Matt and Paul. It was one of the privileges of the job, but it depended on space. As it happened that particular safari was not fully booked, so Phil went ahead and made arrangements. His three guests had already arrived in Kariba town and were looking forward to being part of the five-day safari starting that weekend. Then, at the last minute, the safari company decided to

13

fit in a couple of complimentary guests of their own. There would be no room for Nicky, Matt and Paul. Phil was unhappy at the turn of events, and registered his anger by resigning. This, therefore, would be his last trip down river for that particular company.

There were several different canoe safari outfits operating in those days, some on the Zimbabwe side, others in Zambia. Phil's company had its base camp on the Kafue River in Zambia. Their five-day safaris assembled there and drove down river to the Zambezi by motor boat. Phil's group met at the Kafue camp for an early lunch and light hearted familiarisation – breaking the ice before the real adventure. There were nine of them in all: the two Zimbabwean guests Roger and girlfriend Sandra, plus Phil, a boat driver, and six young German tourists: Gerhard, Mecki, Ferdi, Sabine, Hans and Frank.

While their canoes were being made ready by camp staff they all enjoyed a delicious picnic lunch, lounging comfortably in the shade of the indigenous *Kigelia pinnata* trees, known colloquially as 'sausage trees' for their pendulous sausage-like fruit. Then they boarded the speedboat and began the trip down to the mighty Zambezi.

It was a short and uneventful ride until they approached the confluence of the two rivers where the faster-flowing Zambezi swallows up the waters of the smaller river in a turbulent head-on affair. Swirling waters gave them a boisterous buffeting that made for a more entertaining time, a tiny foretaste of the adrenalin pumping surges to come.

Getting towards midstream of the great river, Phil pointed out the variety of trees crowding the Zimbabwean bank. And as they got nearer they could see an abundance of wildlife not so noticeable on the Zambian shoreline. They had a blurred glimpse of a hippo in the distance as their speedboat headed towards their first stop, the base camp where they would spend the first night. Excitement was in the air as the truth began to sink in that they had well and truly left civilisation far behind. They were looking forward to something new, something fresh, they were saying goodbye to the stresses of their everyday working lives among their own kind.

Forty-five exhilarating minutes later they arrived at Mtondo, their first-night island camp, a comparatively luxurious set-up of dining room, bar, chalets, toilets, showers, riverside deck, and camp fire at night. They were met by porters and shown to their comfortable little tent chalets. Once settled in, they all met on the deck for sundowners. From their splendid perch they were able to relax completely, watching the river flow by and soaking up the atmosphere of the African night. They were a little mystified when Phil promised them a show for later – 'bush TV', he called it.

The 'show' began early. A small herd of elephant wandered into the camp to graze. When one of the younger bulls strayed too close to the toilets Phil moved over to ask him to leave. Normally his presence alone would persuade the youngster to depart, but not so this time. It took quite an exchange of trumpeting and shouting and raving and waving of arms and trunks before the elephant took heed and pushed off with nothing more threatening than a derisory snort. The audience was impressed.

A few drinks by the fireside watching the dancing flames and glowing sparks rising up and drifting away into the night brought the curtain down, and slowly the guests wandered off to their beds to fall asleep to the soft lullaby of the African bush.

Next morning Phil was awake early to check the canoes and their contents, stocking up his cooler-box with ice and cool drinks for the day ahead. Mouth-watering smells wafted through the camp, drawing everyone out of bed for a traditional Zambezi breakfast feast.

Then, before setting off, Phil took the opportunity to set a few ground rules and prepare them a little for what they were likely to encounter.

First of all, the canoes must stick together and travel as a group, with Phil in the lead. For much of the day they would be going through relatively shallow waters and hazards like hippo and crocodiles would usually be easily spotted and avoided. The day would be hot and long, although the paddling would not be over tiring. They would have an occasional opportunity to stop and swim in the shallows whenever he felt it safe. He advised them how to handle a capsize; to stay with the canoe and not try to get back in without help.

Submerged logs and very shallow water were the two most likely causes of capsize, although there was always the outside possibility of a hippo behaving badly.

When everyone was briefed and ready they pushed off into the flowing Zambezi, the current pulling them towards a safari none of them would ever forget.

For the first few kilometres they could stick to the centre of the river in a wide, sluggish section which allowed them to practise some of the paddling skills needed to manoeuvre their canoes around the various obstacles of hidden sandbanks and hippos too lazy or stubborn to get out of the way.

Hippo communities are known as 'pods', and they are as different as groups of people. Phil had got to know many of these pods, and he could predict which were likely to be troublesome and which indifferent to passers-by.

In most parts where the river was narrower Phil would lead the group close to the banks so that the hippos could head into the deeper water where they feel safest and less threatened, while the guests could seek safety on the banks if anything untoward should happen.

They enjoyed a glorious first day of pleasant paddling, quickly settling into an easy rhythm, hardly interrupted by the many hippo pods they passed at a safe distance on their way. At one point when a pod was close enough for them to hear the snorts and grunts, Phil got them all to paddle over to him and join up to make one large floating raft-like mass: a safety measure and deterrent to any prospective underwater intrusion. This

17

joining manoeuvre was known as 'leg-over' because someone in each canoe would put one leg over and into the next canoe to form a kind of close-knit chain.

Once the canoes were linked Phil broke out the cool drinks and passed them around; a welcome treat in the heat of the day. Then, as they neared a shallow section Phil suggested a swim to cool down. They pulled their canoes into the shallows and tied them to paddles stuck in the sand. Phil was first to take a plunge, but soon they were all splashing about happily.

Refreshed, they drifted on again linked by leg, chatting lazily about the scene and no doubt beginning to feel like seasoned Zambezi explorers.

By the time they reached the next camp they had passed dozens of hippo without incident and seen some crocodiles basking on sandbanks or cruising slowly and silently by. Wild Africa may have begun to feel almost tame and safe.

Late in the afternoon they reached camp, tired and ready for a good meal and looking forward to an early bed. Enjoying sundowners by a roaring camp fire they chatted away merrily, recalling every scene from their highly charged day.

Meanwhile, some way downstream at another camp on the banks of the river there was a party of five getting ready for a fishing trip. Alistair Gellately and Arthur Taylor were professional hunters in Zimbabwe. With them were Arthur's wife Faye and her parents, Clive and Brenda Kelly. They were staying at Kingfisher Camp in which Alistair had a part share. It was a trip they had planned for months.

Fate decreed that these two groups should be linked in a bizarre chain of terrifying circumstance.

Phil's group set off early next morning, drifting through a labyrinth of sandbars, confidence increasing with each passing hour as their bodies adjusted to the heat and the easy workload. The day went by relatively unremarkably, except for the ever increasing magnificence of the environment they were so casually passing through.

Camp again, camp fire as usual, early night once more. And so to their fourth day. It was Easter Sunday, just another impossibly beautiful and tranquil sunrise on one of the greatest rivers on earth.

It was another opportunity for drifting lazily along rather than urgent paddling. There was no great hurry, and in any case that was the ideal pace to absorb the very best of the environment's shoreline bird and animal life.

The canoes were spread out five abreast about 30 metres from the Zambian shore, Phil the outer marker. By late morning they were nearing one of his favourite picnic spots where a giant acacia hung over the river to give welcome shade to beach the canoes. It was a good time and place for a lunch break because in the next stage they would have to pass close to a part of the river known to guides as 'Hippo City' because in the deep water there a very large pod of these creatures had taken up permanent residence.

As they approached their lunch stop Phil called all the canoes over to join up in the now familiar "leg over" formation. As he had done on countless safaris before, he secured the nearest canoe, the one in which Gerhard and Mecki were seated, to his by putting his leg into it, thus freeing his hands to dish out drinks from the cooler box. When all five canoes were joined together in like fashion everyone settled back to enjoy the drinks whilst lazily scanning the river banks. The little flotilla drifted peacefully downstream, voices hushed, spirits in harmony.

Suddenly the peace and tranquillity of the moment was rudely shattered.

A huge hippo broke the surface just behind Phil's canoe and closed its jaws on the little craft and the lower part of his right leg. The waters erupted in a frenzied bloody froth knocking Roger and his companion Sandra right out of their canoe.

The rear of Phil's canoe was clamped in the hippo's jaws and seemed to hang there for a few frozen moments before it tilted sideways and capsized. For a few terrifying seconds Phil saw his own reflection in the eye of the beast. He shouted at the others to head for the river bank, at the same time lunging desperately for his paddle, hoping to push himself free. Then he felt himself being pulled overboard and shaken wildly.

"I can still hear Phil screaming as he was dragged beneath the surface time and time again," Sandra remembers.

For Phil the first memory was of his canoe being lifted clear of the water. He thought he must have run onto a sandbank, but the reality quickly took over as he twisted around and came face to face with a wild rampaging hippo. He saw the back end of his canoe perched in the dead centre of the hippo's head. It seemed to hang there before it tilted sideways and capsized.

My immediate reaction was to fight. I lashed out with my free foot and kicked the hippo twice in the mouth and once in the eye. Then I was filled with a sensation of utter calm as I realised that there was little point fighting a two or more ton hippo. I knew I needed to save my breath and energy if I hoped to survive. I relaxed completely and let my body go limp.

The thrashing seemed to go on for an eternity. I remember what seemed like a large black lump attached to me, bubbles blending dark and light green waters in a whipped up frenzy.

I felt no pain, no bones breaking, no tearing muscles; only the whiskers on the monster's chin tickling the skin of my right leg and his lips flapping and beating upon my left.

I was running out of air.

I felt sure I was going to drown.

I could hold on no longer.

Just then I had a floating sensation as if freed from the monstrous grip and allowed to escape unencumbered into the next world. I found myself at the surface of the river.

Was I still alive?

I thought my leg had been ripped right off. I couldn't feel it.

I was bleeding to death and floating in crocodile-infested waters...

Released at last and gasping for air, Phil glanced around and saw to his relief that most of the others had managed to scatter out of the reach of the hippos. He glimpsed his blue paddle floating away on the current, but there was nothing he could do to retrieve it. His upturned canoe was floating nearby and somehow he managed to propel himself towards it and hold on tight, pulling himself parallel to it to confuse any lurking crocs. Hanging on to the canoe he closed his eyes and drifted with it.

Another hippo surfaced nearby and made a few mock sallies at Gerhard's canoe as he and Mecki paddled furiously after Phil. As they drew level with him, they hastily threw the picnic table and chairs which were stored in the front of their canoe into the river to make space for him. Then they began to haul him aboard. The surge of pain was unbearable as the leg he thought he had lost snagged on the side of the canoe, but they eventually managed to get it free and ease him up and in. He crumpled awkwardly into the bottom decking. He was trailing the bloody limb. The canoe slowly began to fill with his blood.

Through a fog of pain Phil heard Mecki's voice which appeared to come to him from far off:

"What the hell do we do now?"

The happy, tight-knit group of only minutes before was now in total disarray, Phil disabled and half-conscious, and the canoes separated all over the place. At any moment another hippo might surface to drive home the attack. They had to make a decision fast. Despite the waves of pain and nausea threatening to overpower him Phil managed to cling to consciousness long enough to grasp the predicament and urge them to seek safety on the river bank. With an immense effort of will he forced himself to stay awake.

The group had been split. Gerhard and Mecki with the injured Phil were now on the far side of a hippo pod, Ferd and the rest had reached the bank on the Zambian shoreline.

It was about 12:30, and the next scheduled radio communication with the company was only at 18:00. Phil needed to get help well before that if possible; his life blood draining away. Aware that there was a safari camp called Chikwenya somewhere nearby on the Zimbabwean side with its own airstrip and radio communications, he managed to communicate this to Gerhard and Mecki and it was agreed they should try to get there.

After a brief shouted exchange, Gerhard and Mecki began paddling with Phil for the Zimbabwean bank four kilometres opposite. The others headed dispiritedly for the Zambian shore which was closest to them, where they would wait until help arrived.

By the time their canoe reached the far shore severe shock had begun to set in and Phil couldn't tell exactly where they were. Was Chikwenya upstream or downstream? He asked Gerhard to follow the bank upstream for about fifteen minutes and then, if he didn't come upon the camp, to try the opposite direction.

Gerhard set off on foot.

Mecki, who was training to be a nurse, then went to work on Phil, draping a wet towel over him to keep him cool, making him drink water, and covering his mangled leg with another towel to avoid distressing him further and to try to staunch the flow of blood..

Gerhard hadn't returned after half an hour so they assumed he had reached the Chikwenya camp and help was being organised. They expected a boat would appear from around the river bend at any moment. But as the long minutes passed with no sign of anyone, exhausted and weak with loss of blood, Phil slipped in and out of consciousness.

When Gerhard did get back an hour and a half later he was wide eyed with terror, white as a sheet and scarcely articulate. It took several minutes for him to calm down and explain what had happened. He told them he had virtually sprinted upstream for about 30 minutes, dodging trees and bushes, and climbing in and out of dry riverbeds. He had found the camp but it was deserted. Desperate to get back as fast as he could, he was just crossing a dry river inlet when he ran into a pride of lions coming down to the river for water. Luckily they were as shocked by the encounter as he was and they quickly moved off back into the bush. But it left him in such a state of shock that he was too frightened now

24

to go downstream to look for another camp. He said he had seen a few vehicles on the Zambian bank and thought it best to get back in the canoe and cross the river to look that side. Frustrated, but in no position to argue, Phil lay back in the canoe, overcome by pain as they pushed off back into the current.

The only thing Gerhard could think of was reaching the vehicles he had seen on the far shore. Phil was willing himself to live and staying positive while the two paddled hard for the shore. After some time he heard stones grazing the underside of the canoe and he wearily raised himself on to his elbows believing they had reached the Zambian shore, only to see they were on an island.

When Gerhard realised the truth they had already lost more precious minutes.

Off they set again, only for the same thing to happen again – there were so many islands dotting the river at that point.

With pain and frustration dragging him down it was difficult for Phil to explain how best to get through the maze of sandbanks and island decoys that blocked their direct route. He wanted to tell Gerhard to stick to the outermost curve of the river where the current was fastest rather than try for the apparently shortest straight line, but the words would not come. And so the little ambulance blundered from sandbar to island and island to sandbar. It seemed to take forever.

Eventually they arrived at the other bank however. During the crossing they had been swept a little downstream by the current and now found themselves near the company camp they were to have reached that evening.

The staff stared aghast at the exhausted three in a canoe awash with blood. It was now about 3.30 pm. and it had been over four hours since the attack. In all that time Phil had had no medication and he was in great pain.

Gerhard was shouting at them to get help, but there was none available. A battered old Land-Rover which more often than not failed to start was all that was there, and Phil didn't fancy his chances of getting to safety in that untrustworthy contraption, so they decided to push on upstream try to reach the vehicles Gerhard had seen.

Much later Phil recalled how he managed to find the strength to hang on in those desperate circumstances.

As he lay in the bottom of the canoe he called on his knowledge of creative visualisation, a technique he had learned as a teenager from his mother, Sally, while she was battling breast cancer.

Meanwhile some distance upstream, soaked to the skin and traumatised by the harrowing experience, the rest of the group had made it to shore. They dragged their canoes onto the bank and sprawled exhausted on the sand.

At first they simply lay there in fear and confusion. Eventually however it began to dawn on them that they were alone with little defence against the late afternoon chill and the wild animals they knew to be all around them. There was a strong likelihood that they would be forced to spend the approaching night where they were.

Slowly they roused themselves from their torpor and began to forage for wood to start a fire. A fire would keep most wild animals at bay. Collecting firewood was no easy task in the thorny scrub along the river bank, particularly as most of them had lost their footwear in the chaos of the hippo attack and aftermath.

A long way further downstream near the Maputa gorge Arthur Gellately and his friends were thoroughly enjoying themselves. They had already passed a couple of days on the river, fishing and later sitting contentedly around the camp fire chatting about the sport they were having. Life on the Zambezi was good.

Upstream, Gerhard and Mecki with Phil on board were finally making real progress. They came upon a Lusaka farmer and his family on a weekend fishing trip in the area. The unexpected arrival of a bloody canoe with two panic-stricken Germans and a young man more dead than alive took them completely by surprise, but they reacted brilliantly.

In minutes the farmer and his family carried the canoe with Phil in it up the steep bank. Placing a mattress next to the canoe they first rolled it over on the opposite side to tip out the bloodied water before tipping it back again and gently sliding Phil onto the mattress. One of the rescuers ripped his shirt into pieces to apply a tourniquet while the others busied themselves finding much needed drinks to ease Phil's suffering. He gladly accepted cold water and a cigarette which seemed to

27

have an analgesic effect. They strapped a paddle to his leg as a makeshift splint.

As woozy as he felt, and in very severe pain, Phil still had wit enough to appreciate what they were doing for him. He marvelled at the generosity and resourcefulness of these people who without hesitation had leapt to his aid.

He was trying to say something of this to them when they all heard the approaching hum of an engine. It was the battered old Land-Rover which the camp staff had somehow coaxed into life.

Phil was quickly loaded aboard and they were soon bouncing down the rough bush track in the direction of the camp, hoping to reach it in time for the scheduled radio contact. Every bump was agony for Phil and he begged the driver to slow down. They reached the camp at six pm, just in time.

The driver leapt out, grabbed the radio handset, hurriedly informed the main camp of the hippo attack and Phil's now critical condition, and asked for emergency evacuation.

The only realistic plan turned out to be to drive on to another fishing camp further upstream. There it was arranged they would be met by a motor boat to get them back to the Mtondo main camp where a plane would be waiting to get Phil to a hospital. Only when the Land Rover returned would the driver, with Gerhardt and Mecki, be able to go back to look for the rest of their original party.

And thus it was that the other six remained stranded on the riverside downstream, helpless, bewildered and shaken, and fearing for their guide's life and their own survival. To add to their anxiety they heard gunshots in the distance after dark. They worried the shooting might mean the presence of poachers; yet another unwelcome threat. But the fire was beginning to blaze away and they were warming up.

Seemingly hours later a different noise caught their attention, the sound of an approaching vehicle. Somebody must have seen their fire. Had it alerted possible poachers to their unwelcome presence? Was it a rescue party? They hardly dared to hope. Their spirits soared when the lights of a vehicle lit up the darkening scrub around them and they heard the voices of Gerhard and Mecki calling out to them. Sure enough, the firelight had guided the camp staff to the stranded party.

The chatter was incessant, it seemed everyone was talking at once; they were all so relieved and happy to be together and safe again that they couldn't stop the garbled recall of fears, feelings, hopes and horrors of what was undoubtedly the longest day in any of their lives.

When all was still again they climbed into the Land-Rover and set off into the darkness bound for Mtondo camp which they were assured was only an hour or so away.

But the affair was not yet over. After travelling for some time it became clear that they were lost.

With fuel running low they decided to conserve what little they had left until it was light enough for the driver to recover his bearings. They would have to spend the night in the bush after all. They felt much safer, however, and they soon had another fire going. If that did not deter nocturnal visitors then they could always retreat to the safety of the vehicle. As they lay around the camp fire that night the conversation was all about Phil: would he survive the mad dash through the bush over the rough tracks they themselves had experienced? From what they had heard from Gerhardt and Mecki no one was optimistic.

In the darkness, some miles ahead of them, Phil's rescue vehicle was crawling along the rough dirt roads that wound through the National Park. The sun had sunk behind the mountains to the west when the silence of the surrounding bush was abruptly shattered by a burst of gunfire. Amid a hail of bullets that showered the vehicle with tree bark and branches the four Zambian camp staff dived on top of Phil for cover. Alarmed, the driver put his foot down hard and they sped off up the road with Phil's agonised cries punctuating their progress.

The source of the gunfire proved to be a trigger-happy anti-poaching squad operating in the National Park. Any vehicle in the park after sunset was presumed to mean illegal entrants and probably poachers. A recent increase in poaching in the area had resulted in a "shoot first ask questions later" policy by guards in the park. Although no one was injured in the incident the already badly injured Phil suffered excruciating agony in the mad dash away from the shooting.

Not long afterwards they arrived at Cumming's fishing camp where they found a group of fishermen and their wives relaxing over a few beers. Their humour and presence were a welcome relief after the sheer terror of the day thus far, but their jolly suggestion that Phil drink as much beer as possible to dull the pain was wisely rejected in favour of more water and Panadol – his first pain relief in over nine hours.

As Phil lay there in great pain, three Italian doctors were boarding a rescue boat 30 kilometres upriver to come to his assistance. They had been on holiday and attending the official opening of a new camp when they heard by radio of Phil's situation. They immediately volunteered to go to his aid. They took two litres of intravenous fluids with them, assuming mistakenly that other basic medical supplies would be available at the base camp.

After setting off they asked for the boat's torch and medical kit. There was no torch, and the battered tin can that passed for a medical kit contained only a few gauze bandages and a couple of plasters. The boat driver assured them there was no need for a torch as there was more than enough moonlight and in any case he knew the way.

About twenty minutes into the journey and travelling at high speed they slammed into a sandbank and were all violently thrown forward, ending up in a pile at the front of the boat. Badly shaken, but luckily with only a few

31

bruises, they had to climb out on to the sandbank to dislodge the boat to continue on their way. They were aware that time was of the essence, every second critical to Phil's chances of survival - more than ten hours had now passed since the incident and he must be in a bad state.

Getting the boat off the sandbank in the darkness was hard work but they managed it and jumped back in. This time the boat driver proceeded at a more sensible pace.

They continued in darkness for another twenty minutes or so until a second sandbank put an end to their journey. This time they were well and truly stuck. Try as they might they could not get the boat back into deep enough water to continue.

One of the doctors had a flash of inspiration and used her penlight torch to send an SOS signal off into the dark towards the river bank.

Miraculously the signal was spotted by some fishermen on the river bank.   And they immediately came to investigate. With their help the boat was soon back in the water and on its way.

Three hours later they arrived at the camp to find Phil in the back of the Land Cruiser belonging to a kind fisherman. He had given up hope of their arrival and decided that Mtondo camp where they had stayed on the first night of the canoe trip was his best bet. The doctors were horrified at the state Phil was in. Realising they were not adequately equipped to deal with his injuries they did the best they could. They set to work hooking him up to the drips they had brought with them.

32

His veins were so flat as a result of the massive loss of blood that looking for somewhere to insert the needle for the drip was quite a mission. Phil also remembers a female surgeon repeating over and over the worrying news: *"You don't have any blood, your veins are flat!"*

They too had quickly realised that another trip back upriver was out of the question. It was far safer to travel by road and, as Phil was already in the back of the Land Cruiser, they set to work administering the drips they had brought with them. On the journey one of the camp staff had to hang on to the outside of the vehicle to keep the bag of IV fluids high enough to be effective and to shield it from damage as they drove through the bush in the dark. En route the doctors explained how the message had come through too late for a plane to fly in from Lusaka but that one would arrive first thing in the morning to fly him out.

Bruno Piotti, one of the Italian doctors in the group, recalls the dire situation that awaited them at the camp when they finally reached it:

"Phil was in serious shock due to massive haemorrhage when we got to him. His pulse was fast and weak and he was barely able to respond to questions with hand signals. His left leg was badly smashed from his femur down and his lower leg was cold. His first and second toes had already turned black. We could feel no pulse in his foot or ankle. His leg was immobilised between two canoe oars and some strips of cloth held this rudimentary splint together. There was a tourniquet applied to his upper thigh which began to

33

bleed as soon as we touched it. We decided not to move him any more than was necessary as he was stable for the time being. We had two litres of IV drips and one small needle which we set up in his arm to give him the fluids he so desperately needed. On the way to the main camp we stopped at another smaller camp to see if they had any more medical supplies. To our amazement the camp staff brought out more Band-Aids! However, one of the guests at the camp happened to have a first aid kit given to him by a medical rep in Lusaka and which, fortunately for us, his wife had stuck in his bag before he left for a fishing trip. It contained two more litres of IV fluids and kit, a bottle of plasma expander and antibiotics. It was still not adequate for what Phil required but it was a miracle all the same."

After another two long hours they reached the main camp where they put Phil in a tent and did their best to keep him alive, staying by his side throughout the night to monitor his critical signs and give what assistance they could.

Shortly after first light Phil was carried to the camp airstrip, an erstwhile elephant path, and they waited anxiously for the promised rescue plane. After another agonisingly long wait they heard the throb of an engine, and a light aircraft landed and taxied slowly down the rough, dung-covered track to where they were all waiting. They cursed inwardly as they saw that the double-door aircraft they had requested had not materialised. This made the task of getting Phil aboard excruciatingly painful. Even after unbolting the seats it

34

was with great difficulty that they manoeuvred his stretcher into the small plane, the IV falling out onto the dusty, runway several times in the process.

They were even more alarmed when it was revealed that the requested clearance for a direct flight to Harare had been refused. This meant Phil would have to be flown first to Kariba with inevitable bureaucratic red tape – he had lost all his identification papers when his canoe capsized. One of the doctors just managed to squeeze into the plane and they took off for Kariba just after 9am., every jolt on the rough runway entailing further agony for the stricken Phil. The others were to follow them later by road.

In Kariba, an anxious Nicky waited for news of her brother. She had heard of the attack and rushed straight to the safari company office for news. Little information was available other than that he would be flown into Kariba that morning. With her two companions, Paul and Matt, she headed out for the small airport.

When they arrived they desperately sought officials who could give them an idea of what was happening but they were met by hostility and apparent indifference. In fact the customs officials seemed more concerned about the fact that they had no identification.

After enduring what seemed like hours of red tape with officials completing unnecessary forms Nicky glanced out of the window and noticed a small plane on the tarmac around which some people were standing and gesticulating, obviously engaged in a heated argument.

She knew instinctively that it was Phil, and that she had to get to him regardless of the consequences.

Having flown in and out of it on numerous occasions for family camping and fishing trips she was familiar with the layout of the airport and so, as they followed yet another official to his office in a smaller terminal to the left of the main building, she seized her chance. Slipping though the main doors she dashed around the service area where the main gates to the runway were open and unmanned, fear for Phil lending her wings.

She sped across the tarmac to where a small dark-haired woman stood next to the plane she had glimpsed from the window. The woman introduced herself as the doctor who had been caring for Phil since the previous night. She explained that he was in a critical condition. Later Nicky recalled the sight that met her eyes when she climbed into the small plane.

I found Phil on the floor, his head propped up on a makeshift pillow. I couldn't believe they had managed to get him in there, He was lying with his head in the rear of the plane and his legs pressed up against the front seats. His green T-shirt was ripped and covered in dried blood. The cabin was unbearably hot and the stench in the plane was awful. I realised with a shock that it was the smell of rotting flesh. I held his hand tightly and tried to force back the tears. He smiled then, that big, handsome, green-eyed brother of mine and, in a strange reversal of roles considering the circumstances, tried to comfort me.

"Don't worry Nick," he said. It' will be OK. I'll be fine. You'll see."

All I could do was to tell him I loved him before being unceremoniously dragged from the plane by an irate customs official.

"Where are your identification papers? You are illegally on the plane! You come with us! We arrest you!"

Luckily the doctor intervened at this point and the officials calmed down. Nicky took tearful leave of Phil, promising him that she would be in Harare as soon as she could and would try and get a message to their mother, Sally, who was away in the Matopos near Bulawayo for the long weekend and was not expected back until late that night. Cell phones were not common in those days so there was little she could do until Sally returned to Bulawayo.

They drove back to their hotel and made a long-distance call to Harare to tell a close family friend and alert her to Phil's imminent arrival in Harare. Then they checked out in record time and raced back to Harare.

On that same Monday morning, after motoring up through the gorge in search of a prime fishing spot, Arthur cut the engine on their boat, letting it drift slowly back towards the mouth of the gorge from which they had just come.

A few lines trailed from the boat as they drifted out in the middle of the river, watching a small herd of elephants on the far bank and revelling in the primitive beauty of the scene. Without any warning the boat was rocked violently from below. They were all thrown off balance as the bow lifted up into the air and the next instant they were flying into the stern in a tangled heap of arms and legs. Before they could regain their footing the boat was rammed again and this time it capsized, plunging them all head first into the dark Zambezi current. Before they hit the water Alistair caught a fleeting glance of their assailant, a lone hippo, who snorted contemptuously and sank back to whence he had come without so much as a backward glance.

Floundering in the water, the group clung together for a few minutes looking desperately around for a way out of their predicament. The elderly Kellys were not strong swimmers and were having difficulty staying afloat. Arthur had spotted a sandbank not too far away and, between them, he and Faye managed to pull Brenda towards its relative safety. Exhausted, they finally reached the sandbank. They staggered through the shallows to get away from the water's edge to dry sand where crocodiles would hopefully be less inclined to come after them.

Meanwhile Alistair and Clive clung desperately to the capsized boat and managed to climb aboard the upturned hull in an initial attempt to escape the water. Once assured of the safety of his wife and mother-in-law and having regained his breath, Arthur dived back into the river and swam out to the boat where, with Alistair's help, he managed to get Clive back to the sandbank. Before long the whole group was safely huddled in the centre of the tiny sandy island.

It was midday and their situation was not good. They were in a very remote section of the river with very little traffic. They had only two choices: wait for help where they were or try swim to the greater safety of the shore where they could search for help.

Alistair decided to swim for help. There was a fishing camp about 5 kilometres away and if he swam to the bank he could run there and get help. He knew the swim could cost him his life but he had little alternative. It was either that or be at the mercy of the crocodiles which would surely come. He was also the only single man in the party. He dived into the river and headed for the bank 200 metres away.

He covered the distance fairly quickly, but the bank was steep and he couldn't get up it.

A little way upstream he saw an inlet where the banks seemed less sheer and he could get out more easily. After a short swim he entered the still waters and quickly made his way towards a section of the bank which seemed less steep. For a few minutes he lay gasping in the shallows, sapped of energy, trying to summon the strength to drag himself up the bank.

He struggled to his knees and was about to stand up when he saw the distinctive long, scaly head of an enormous crocodile break the surface a few feet from him. As it lunged at him he managed to duck sideways and avoid the snapping jaws.

He saw the croc turn and then circle round him before sinking ominously under the surface once more.

Terrified, he lashed out with his feet and punched at every shadow in the dark waters. Undeterred, the croc shot out of the depths at him, again miraculously missing him by inches as he twisted and turned and beat the water to create confusion.

Again it approached, but this time more slowly.

In the next attack it got him at the elbow of his right arm and began to drag him under water, twisting and turning all the time. Momentarily loosening its grip, Alistair took the chance to fight back, desperately searching with his good left hand for the eye of the monster. He plunged his thumb in and dug at it for all his strength would allow. As it tried to shake him off he thrust his good arm down its throat, clawing at the soft flesh and causing the epiglottis to open for a moment, long enough for water to rush into its lungs. The croc immediately released him and retreated, leaving him gurgling and spluttering but still miraculously alive.

He pulled himself toward a small rocky outcrop with his good arm and, in the shallower water, tried to wash his wounds as best he could. His shoulder was dislocated, his right arm was definitely broken and the flesh was badly mutilated. He knew the wounds would be infected with extremely toxic bacteria and would become gangrenous if he didn't act fast. Ripping his shirt and applying a light tourniquet he staunched the severe bleeding and stumbled weakly up the bank in search of an ant's nest. As a professional hunter he knew that these small insects were invaluable in the treatment of wounds. Coming across a nest he fell down upon it

40

pushing his arm against a broken section crawling with ants. They swarmed all over the mutilated limb and slowly began to clean up the dying flesh in the open wounds. Their small bites releasing formic acid, a natural antiseptic.

Alistair lay there in a daze of exhaustion and pain, and lost consciousness.

When he came to it was late afternoon. Although disorientated by pain and shock he remembered his friends stuck on the sandbank, but he was helpless to do anything but murmur a quiet prayer for their safety. Then he crawled towards a small rocky outcrop nearby, gathering up a few loose stones with which to protect himself from the many predators like lions, leopard and hyena that lived in the area.

A strong breeze was coming in off the river and the chill combined with the shock of his horrific encounter was making him shake uncontrollably. He tried to curl up to conserve his body warmth but the pain surging through his arm made that difficult. The ants were still swarming over his arm and their bites kept him awake, reminding him to loosen the tourniquet every once in a while to keep the blood flow regulated so he didn't starve his lower arm and end up losing it.

Suddenly he was startled by snapping twigs in the bush off to his right.

A fully-grown adult male buffalo pushed his large head and curved horns through the scrub and stared straight at him. Alistair was well aware of just how dangerous a

41

situation he was now in. A lone buffalo can be a cantankerous and highly unpredictable beast.

Somehow he managed to quell his shaking body and stay completely still.

The buffalo snorted, lowered its head and started to charge him. But then another miracle happened. As if sensing something amiss, it stopped short, dropped its head and huge set of horns to sniff at this unmoving thing. Sensing no immediate threat it turned and followed the blood trail down to the water's edge, its huge head rocking to and fro.

Its curiosity satisfied, it retraced its steps up the bank to where he was lying, promptly grunted heavily and lay down beside him with a deep sigh.

Alastair was utterly astounded. The huge beast appeared to have appointed itself his protector. He had never heard of such a thing. But whatever the motives of this massive beast it made him feel less alone in this wild and unforgiving place. His feeling that it was there to protect him was confirmed when throughout the night the buffalo would charge off into the bush snorting and stomping around in the undergrowth before returning to his side.

Throughout the night, not too far away, Alistair could hear the mournful howls of hyenas in the darkness. He was grateful for the bulky presence of his protector and it gave him hope that he might yet survive to rescue his friends. He slipped into a restless sleep.

On the sandbank, meanwhile, the afternoon wore on with no sign of rescue and his stranded friends imagined the worst. Alistair hadn't made it and that meant they were in big trouble.

Huddled together, they kept a constant lookout for crocs. Every ripple and swish of the current was cause for anxiety. A sense of despondency settled over them, fears over the fate of their friend compounded by the knowledge that they had little chance of surviving a night.

But then, just as the dying rays of the sun striped the surface of the water, Arthur noticed something floating just out in the current, and his spirits soared as he realised what it was.

It was a blue paddle.

Quick as he could he waded out and grasped it as it drifted by.

It was a sturdy enough paddle, well-made of fibreglass, about two metres long with a grip on one end. Here was a tool! A weapon to help ward off attack.

It was Phil's paddle, the one he was using when his canoe was attacked upstream earlier that day. Of course no one had any idea of the drama behind that simple piece of flotsam, but they were grateful to have it to help them through the night.

An early full moon illuminated the pitiful scene of survivors clinging to each other around Arthur and the paddle. Every now and then he beat the water, hoping that the gunshot-like sound would keep the crocs away. Fear kept them all wide awake and vigilant throughout the night.

There was much to fear, and over the hours they lost track of the number of crocs that approached and had to be beaten off. For each one they were ready, thrashing the water and screaming at the top of their voices in the only defence available. It worked, and as the sun rose they finally began to hope and have some confidence in their chances of survival.

Back on the riverbank, a few miles upstream, Alistair awoke to the throbbing pain of his mangled shoulder and torn muscles. He carefully raised himself up to a sitting position. There was a sudden crash in the bushes off to his right and he saw the fast disappearing rear of his protector and sleeping companion. Duty done, it was making itself scarce. Strangely enough, its departure left him feeling quite bereft and vulnerable again. But he was alive, and he wondered if his companions too had survived the night. There was no point in going back, he needed to press on to find help.

He stumbled on upriver, keeping close to the river bank, anxious to cover as much distance as quickly as possible.

An hour or so later, and unknown to him, another party of safari canoeists came upon the bedraggled group of survivors on the sandbank in midstream. What a sight they presented; close to tears of relief, with the harrowing experience etched visibly upon their exhausted faces. Space was quickly found for them and they were paddled downriver to the next rendezvous point and safety. There they radioed in the situation and sent out an alert concerning the missing Alistair. They made enquiries too about the possibility that another group might lie stricken upstream – the life-saving paddle being evidence of something, though no one could yet know what.

It was about the same time that Alistair spotted some fishermen across the river on the Zimbabwean shore and he waved wildly to them. All they could see was a strange and bedraggled apparition with torn rags wrapped around one arm. They waved back in relaxed camaraderie unaware at first that he needed help. When he collapsed and lay unmoving on the bank they realised that something was amiss and swiftly came to the rescue. They took him back across the river to the Zimbabwean side and to a nearby bush airfield where they radioed for a plane to fetch him.

In Bulawayo Sally and Pip Longden were returning from their weekend in the Matopos National Park. They knew Phil was on a canoeing trip on the Zambezi and that Nicky had been going to join him. They weren't worried; Phil was a great guide and Nicky was in good hands.

As she walked in the door of their Bulawayo home the phone was ringing. Eager for news of her scattered offspring she picked up the phone. It was Helen, her friend in Harare.

There was no way to break the news gently.

"It's Phil. He's been badly injured in a hippo attack. He is alive, but they are amputating his leg right now."

Stunned, she took a few seconds to register the awful news.

Then she whispered calmly to herself:

"He's all right...he's alive...he's a fighter...he is alright, he's alive, he's a fighter. He will get through this."

Crocodile Fever

June Watt.

A record of adventure in Malawi during the 1950's, telling of the lives of June and her husband Jeff Stutchbury as they set out to seek their fortunes as crocodile hunters on Lake Nyassa. Ill equipped and with no experience, the life was hard but exciting.

At last the planning, experimenting, the correspondence and the Nyasaland Police Force were behind us. We were on the train to Salima. Ahead lay adventure and, we firmly believed, enormous wealth. Giddy with anticipation we chatted, mindless of the torrential rain and deaf to the thunder booming above the shudder and rattle of the train. Our crates containing rifles, ammunition, coarse salt, a primus stove, rope, nails, torches, a little food and medicine were all safely in the goods van.

Hand in hand we alighted at Salim. On enquiring about onward travel to Lilongwe, we were assured that the native bus was the only option available. Nothing daunted, we spent a comfortable night at the unpretentious local hotel. We woke early, eagerly awaiting the bus which was to take us closer to our destination.

Though I kept silent, my first glance at the dilapidated apparition, its roof piled high with an assortment of shabby luggage, crates of dried fish, live chickens in wicker cages, and bicycles, did not inspire confidence.

47

But there was no turning back. Inside, the passengers packed as tightly as sardines in a tin, chatted and laughed raucously. One or two transistor radios blared with gusto.

The driver, a burly man with a gleaming white smile, invited us to join him in the cab. Enormously relieved, we clambered aboard, Jeff placing himself next to the driver. My relief was short lived as the window on the passenger side was broken, letting the rain pour in, soaking and chilling my left side. We swapped seats. This proved to have its own down side. The big cheerful talkative man I was pressed up against, reeked of cheap tobacco, unwashed clothes and last week's perspiration.

The road was a black slithery track. We lurched along changing seats every time we screeched to a halt in a shower of mud to collect another drenched, heavily laden passenger. Seven hours later, nauseous, cold and hungry, we arrived in Lilongwe. Rain still bucketed down. Leaving Jeff to organise the storage of our belongings, I dashed barefoot into the Hotel reception. Strange were the looks I got from the elderly, perfectly coiffed receptionist as I awaited her attention.

"Yes?" she finally said, her blue shadowed lids drooping as she gazed at the pool that was forming about my feet.

"A room for my husband and me", I tried to smile.

"Your husband?" she said, and may as well have added that she recognised a runaway when she saw one.

"Yes" I flushed, "he'll be here in a moment".

Just then Jeff came blustering through the door. The dinner gong sounded as we were escorted to room number twenty two.

I rummaged through our overnight case and found a creased voile dress.

"My shoes" I almost wept "I've left them on the bus!"

"You've got the prettiest feet in the world" Jeff laughed, "give these chaps the privilege of seeing them".

Clutching Jeff's arm I crept into the dining room like a thief but left there well satisfied and with my self-esteem somewhat restored.

Over coffee in the lounge we met a jovial, loud mouthed travelling salesman named Guy who offered us a lift to Kota Kota. This was in spite of the fact that a prominently displayed notice informed guests that the road was impassable.

"Not to worry about that" Guy said waving an indifferent hand, "we'll pass the impassable". We accepted without a qualm.

All I remember about the trip was that we seemed to be aboard an amphibious craft which slithered just above ground all the way to Kota Kota. We finally stopped with a jolt and a piercing screech in front of a large rondavel with a sign reading 'Government Resthouse' emblazoned over the door.

The rest house was nothing more than a large rondavel with braai facility and long-drop outside. Furnishings were Spartan - two beds, two deck chairs and a small cupboard containing a few items of tinned food.

We hired a bicycle and pedalled to the lagoon which flowed from the lake. Here we came across an old hunter trapping crocodiles with a snare made from strong rope, set partly in the water and baited with goat meat. In horrified fascination we questioned him. He explained with comic demonstration how the crocodile would slip through the noose, devour the meat and then be quite unable to reverse. He would then bludgeon the reptile to death. I shuddered. But this was the wilderness, there was no room for squeamishness, as Jeff gently reminded me.

Further along the lagoon a number of children were paddling knee deep. Alarmed, we enquired if this was safe. The old hunter smiled placidly and assured us that he'd put special 'muti' (medicine) on their legs and no crocodile would touch them.

Jeff had gone off to arrange a house. I was trying to envisage what he could have put together in the three days he'd been away when Guy pitched up in his Land Rover to take me there; three interminably long days as I waited restlessly in the rondavel which served as accommodation for the rare visitor to Kota Kota.

When much later Guy brought his Land Rover to a halt where the road petered out, we were in front of a tiny derelict building crouched beneath two small trees. On one mud-spattered wall, bold whitewash proclaimed that this was Saidi's Cash Store. Without ceremony, Guy had hauled my effects from the vehicle, dumped them at my feet and informed me that bearers had been selected.

"Those chaps", he said pointing to ten black men lolling in the shade. He leapt back into the Land Rover and spun around.

"Happy hunting" he smiled as the vehicle lurched away in a vortex of grey dust.

Ill at ease, aware of the many curious eyes watching me, I entered the dark coolness of the store. Bags of dried beans and sugar sagged against peeling walls. Small tins of jam, fish and fruit adorned a few rickety shelves. Pen knives, candles and earrings mingled in a grimy glass case. I asked for cigarettes. The Indian owner introduced himself, told me that he'd met Jeff, and handed me a packet of ten 'Tom-Tom' cigarettes. "They're a bit harsh" he said "but it's all I have".

Five hundred and seventy miles by eighty miles of magnificent water covering one fifth of the country rumbled somewhere to the left of me. A dozen small tributaries drained through tangled brush into the marsh flanking the lake. But none of this concerned me as I followed the ten porters, crates and boxes held high, the murmur of the water clear above the deep chanting of the men.

We had walked for close to an hour when the bearers, their voices joined in rhythmic song, veered towards the lake. Gradually the scrubby bush gave way to surprisingly soft white sand.

A Kingfisher rose from some secret place, hovered like a pirouetting ballerina and plummeted into the water. Waves rose, splintered onto the hot sand and raced back, gentle as scurrying kittens. A fish eagle called, piercing the sun bleached sky. My heart did something irregular under the damp khaki on my back. I tightened my grip on the .22 hanging from my shoulder. Suddenly, I was afraid. The beach lay frighteningly before me, an endless white nothingness, going nowhere. I trudged on. The porters chanted. The lake rose and fell unceasingly. My eyes burned.

Far away, oh so far away, a tiny shadow blotted the virgin sand. Nothing moved. I blinked. Could it be a rock, a mirage? My stomach curled tight. Dread beat like small drums at my temples. Where was Jeff? Moments passed, slow and hot. Courage seeped away in the perspiration damping my palms. I was suddenly aware that I was one woman in the company of ten black fishermen most of whom, I found out later, had never seen a white woman.

A shape broke from the shadow. Strong brown legs moved swiftly towards us. A voice boomed above the noise of the waves. Jeff! I hurtled past the astonished porters, sand filled my takkies, wind took my hat, the .22 banged against my hip. He was really here. We reached each other.

"Dr Livingstone" I gasped. He laughed with relief, lifted me off my feet and there, with me hanging from his neck like a rag doll, he danced a little jig.

Still chanting, the bearers heaped our baggage in and around our hut, cupped their hands as Jeff paid them, and away they ambled across the sand waving, smiling and wishing us well.

Inside, two deck chairs, a few upturned boxes, rope hanging from nails, rifles resting against thatch, cool sand underfoot.

"This is wonderful" I told Jeff, relieved to be out of the broiling sun.

"Your mansion Madam" he mocked with a little bow.

"I thank you good sir" I said stripping off my gun-belt and takkies, finding the primus stove.

"Time for tea. Sorry no cucumber sandwiches today"

The rest of the afternoon was spent prising open boxes and crates finding space for everything. By nightfall, exhausted, we ate tinned beans and sausage, rolled ourselves in blankets and lay down on the sand. I watched stars peeping brazenly through the thin thatch, listened to the twitter of nightjars, the hesitant croak of frogs and the endless lap of water on the beach.

Towards morning I woke. Something was crawling up my limbs. I flicked on the torch. Ticks! Four of them. Little flat brown crawly things sucking my blood. I screamed, plucked them off and shuddering with horror, squashed them into eternity. Weeks later I would be able to pull them off and toss them onto the sand with total indifference.

Jeff, I always maintained, was a descendant of Heath Robinson. He broke up a crate and built a table around the thick centre pole supporting the roof of our hut. A smaller box was curtained and turned into a grocery cupboard. He constructed an amazing toilet complete with wooden seat and surrounded it with a flimsy grass wall. The problem was that the seat was so high and the wall so low that I could survey the landscape from where I sat.

"You built the seat for yourself and the wall for me" I accused him.

He laughed a lot but never changed it.

A bathroom was added to the main room where jug and basin rested on a slatted bamboo shelf. Nails hammered into the poles were used as hooks on which to hang towels and clothes.

Our evening routine was to light a Hurricane lamp and place it close to the water's edge. We'd then wade in and splash wildly, in our ignorance, believing that this would scare away any lurking reptile, before venturing deeper for our nightly bath. To dry off we ran naked on the beach.

We fished daily, often catching more than we needed. These delicious bream, known locally as Chambo, we either grilled on an open fire outdoors or on the Primus inside." We would fish from separate rocky outcrops about five hundred yards apart vying with each other as to the number caught. Then we would walk towards one another pretending to be strangers, calling out greetings like,

"How's the fishing your end?"

"Join me for a gin and tonic at my hotel"

And we'd laugh and kiss in the sun.

From time to time we would visit Saidi's store to replenish paraffin, sugar and matches and occasionally, a tin of jam which we ate by the spoonful having no bread to spread it on. The village adjoined the store so we would go there to buy eggs, rice and sometimes a scrawny chicken. The sellers would often prefer to barter their goods for salt.

When we ran out of tea our cook showed us how a spoonful of sugar, burned to a deep brown, boiling water poured over and stirred rapidly, was an acceptable substitute. When we ran out of cooking oil, we simply laid the fish over the coals. On one occasion, with nothing but eggs in the larder, I ate five boiled eggs at one sitting. I made vetkoek with a mixture of ordinary flour and kasava flour. We tried the kasava on its own but it was so astringent that it was better to go hungry. Eventually our diet was reduced to fish, eggs, a little rice and plantains.

Women would frequently come to our hut hungry for salt, bringing eggs and chickens to barter. Long hours were spent carefully measuring a cupful of salt in exchange for two eggs, six cups for a chicken. I would place the eggs in a pot full of water to check their freshness. If they floated they were old, if they remained on the bottom they were fresh. The women would argue the point, often claiming that they were laid that very day. To prove them wrong I would break an egg. After this there would be much clapping of hands over astonished mouths, mutterings and shrugging.

The men fished, made and repaired nets. I never knew them to do anything else. Once they'd brought home their daily quota of fish, they would sit, legs outstretched, in the sun smoking and chatting. The women did such chores as they deemed necessary.

They would cook, strip, soak and lay kasava root on the rocks and when dry, stamp them into meal. They would feed and scold the children. The men would only rise when called for dinner.

While in Saidi's store one day, he told us that his brother had a boat and outboard engine for sale. On hearing the price, we decided that it would be worth delving into our small capital to acquire such an asset. Before dawn the next day we set off with two bearers, optimistically calculating that we would take no more than eight hours to cover the twenty two miles to Kota Kota. We took along only the rifles, some hard boiled eggs and drinking water.

The beach was soon behind us. We passed through the village where men lazed about in the early morning sun before setting off for the day's fishing. Women were busy pounding kasava root, children darted about squealing with delight at seeing the Muzungu (White people). We waded through rice paddies, across stony areas into the scant bush.

Before long we were confronted by a fast flowing stream, about thirty feet wide. Two small trees had collapsed and lay close together across it. Jeff handed me the rifles and carefully tested their strength. They held his weight.

Laughing and slapping the terrified porters on the shoulders, he managed to convince them that it was safe enough to cross using the tree trunks as a bridge. He followed and hailed me from the opposite bank.

I would like it known that I have an inordinate fear of water and am a very poor swimmer. It took every last scrap of courage for me to cross the thirty feet, making my way hand over foot, looking down into the swirling yellow water below. When I finally reached the bank I quite literally let go and flung myself into the slushy black mud. Jeff gave me a hand up with a hearty chuckle, whether in relief that I'd made it or amusement at the sight I presented I will never know.

On we went, occasionally meeting a very surprised traveller. We rested a while, ate some eggs, and continued. Fatigue set in. We'd been walking for eight hours. Just then, with my enthusiasm rapidly waning, we were confronted by another stream, wider than the first Clusters of weed swayed in the fast flowing current. There were no conveniently fallen tree trunks this time. There was however one thick branch protruding from a big tree, about three feet above the surface of the stream. Again, Jeff handed me the rifles and waded in to test the depth. It reached his collar bones. My heart sank. He positioned himself under the bough, motioned to me to clamber along the branch and then drop onto his shoulders. My heart flipped but, with no other choice, I slung the rifles over my shoulders, tightened the revolver about my waist, tied my takkies together and hung them around my neck. With trembling legs, and hands damp with anxiety, I managed the feat. To this day my scalp crawls when I recall the moment I looked down into the rushing water with Jeff's shoulders below me, praying feverishly that I'd land on them and not in the yellow water.

Day was dwindling. We stopped talking and slogged wearily on. Hope sprang anew when we came across a local dressed in European clothing. Surely Kota had to be close now. We enquired how much further to our destination. It took some time for him to understand the question, his English being very poor. With a shrug and a perplexed frown came the reply.

"No miles, Sir. Maybe two days by footing".

Two days! Had we walked in a circle?

"Oh no, no, no" I almost cried.

"I don't think he understood" Jeff said trying to comfort me.

Hope had evaporated like mist in the sun. Silent with disappointment we staggered hopelessly on.

The sun had rolled away. Dusk had fallen. In the far distance we spotted a few lamp lights twinkling. Kota was in sight. Our everlasting walk was coming to a close. I sat down on the hard ground. Only now did I become aware of just how painful my feet were. Blisters covered the entire ball of each foot. After a short rest I was unable to stand up again. Helpless tears burned hot behind my eyes. Jeff hauled me onto his back and carried me the last few hundred yards to the rest house where I collapsed on the bed and slept till the sun crept into the rondavel and woke me.

Having bought the boat and engine plus a few groceries, Guy again did the honours, giving us a lift, and in no time we were outside Saidi's store. I marvelled at the miracle of the wheel and combustion engine as I kissed Guy on the cheek.

Porters were hastily found to convey our new possessions to the hut where Jeff immediately set about checking the boat for leaks. He found several. Working tirelessly he repaired them with strips of hessian and bitumen. Watching this I had a vision of speeding across the lake, leaving behind our trusty but cumbersome canoe.

Most days we hunted crocodiles. Set noose traps. Waited in the ever blazing heat of the sun on outcrops of rock jutting from the water. Waiting silently for the flat dark heads to break the surface. Then fire and paddle furiously to grab the carcass before it sank. Many a day we returned to camp empty handed. Once in his eagerness and haste to take a shot, Jeff laid his rifle barrel on my shoulder to steady himself, and fired. The shot deafened me bursting my eardrum and inflicting a great deal of pain.

My ear ached abominably. Desperate, I tried an old remedy passed down to me from my Grandmother. Hot salt in a small bag held to the offending ear.

For days I went about with this clutched to my head in between taking painkillers. There was little improvement.

Guy had told us that a medical orderly called at Kota once a fortnight. Hoping that he was available, we sent a runner to the village. Two days later we learned that he was at Saidi's store and decided to collect him by boat. I was, as usual armed with two saucepans with which to bail out the boat as water rushed in through holes Jeff had not been able to repair. At the sight of these, the orderly, a tall, very thin young man, enquired nervously

"What are those for?"

"To bail out the water" I told him casually, accustomed as I was to this necessary duty.

"Oh my" he whimpered, gripping the sides of the boat as Jeff got the outboard going.

At the hut he announced that I'd developed an infection, and gave me a large penicillin injection.

"I can't come back you see." he smiled thinly.

.....

A short distance from camp a narrow but deep stream flowed into the Lake. Jeff with his usual imaginative mind, dreamed up the idea of spanning a baited net across it.

"We could easily lure two or more croc that way," he said.

"Where in the world would we get a net that size?" I asked.

"Come", he smiled.

I followed him to the village where he explained to an attentive fisherman, what was required. Soon the patient Nyasa fishermen commenced plaiting strips of inner bark, working diligently from sunrise to sunset. Two weeks later the mammoth task was complete.

Duly baited with goat meat and secured at either side of the stream, the rope net device stretched out like a hammock across the gurgling water.

We waited till the sun had slipped away, stowed the rifles, torch and canoe in the sheltering water-weed and waited. Night fell. A million mosquitoes found their way up cuffs, down collars, and stung through khaki drill. Still we sat silent in the darkness. Time passed slowly. Toward morning, not able to endure the maddening insects any longer, I had just decided to go back to camp when the stream was suddenly whipped into a thrashing whirlpool.

"The torch" hissed Jeff.

I snapped it on, training the beam onto the water. Two crocodiles were trapped in the net. Twisting and leaping they raged against the obstruction. Jeff raised the rifle to his shoulder, moving the barrel in a small arc as he tried to take aim. As his finger curled around the trigger, a huge splutter, a heave of scaly backs and the pair broke free. In a moment the stream lay calm. I doused the torch. Jeff stood stock still for a long moment, rifle limp in his hand.

"Damn it", he finally muttered.

Very softly from the opposite bank Nason started singing a tuneless lament. Mulenga joined, their voices in complete harmony with the small night sounds of Africa. Shrill little chirpings, all but inaudible stirring of leaf and nocturnal wing, the incessant lap lapping of waves breaking on the sand.

"Pull her up", Jeff spoke quietly.

There at five am we beheld what was left of a great idea. A heap of tangled bark glimmering in the pale morning light. Bone weary and crestfallen we walked slowly back to the hut.

Crouched over a small fire, slapping at mosquitoes, we were having a few bananas and black tea for supper. A white moon hung low over silver-plated incessantly lapping water. From afar, two bobbing lights appeared amongst the scrub. Silenced by surprise, fear and curiosity, we watched. The flares came closer, brighter. I felt for the Colt at my hip, noticed Jeff shifting closer to the rifle lying beside him.

Two tall men, naked but for the tiny loin cloths about their hips, bodies glowing with perspiration, jogged into camp bearing yard long flaming torches fashioned from some tightly twisted stuff. They stopped where Nason and Mulenga sat on their haunches close to their own small fire, communicated softly with much gesticulating, words that we did not understand. Mulenga detached himself from the foursome.

"They say their boss man he tell you to come eat at his house", he said smiling in the firelight. We questioned him closely being quite suspicious. What boss? A white man? How far away was he? Mulenga exchanged further unintelligible words with the torch bearers.

"Him Indian man. House near", he informed us.

Bush telegraph had been busy. Jeff and I exchanged glances. Should we take a chance? Was this a ruse to rob us? Our trepidation was overcome by our young appetites. We could not resist the thought of a good meal. We decided to go.

We followed stumbling along in silence behind the loping messengers, each secretly afraid of an ambush. After about half an hour the re-assuring glow of a lamp from a small window set in a smudge of whitewashed wall. A house. It was all right. Someone really had invited us to dinner.

The master of the ramshackle abode, a sloe-eyed, middle-aged Indian, greeted us in pidgin English, invited us to sit on a bed, the only furniture in the room apart from a low stool. Leaning against the opposite wall, six or eight black men sat cross legged watching our every move.

Our host provided huge helpings of delicious egg curry, followed by sweet ripe paw paw and strong black tea. We tried to make conversation but the Indian's English was so poor all we got in response was,

"Yes, yes, very good".

After an hour we expressed our thanks and indicated that we were ready to leave.

"No, no" our host said making it clear that he wanted us to spend the night. He bade us a grudging farewell, turned into his house without the offer of an escort.

Staggering through the bush with the light of the moon and the sound of breaking water our only guide, it took a long time for us to reach camp, there to find our staff snugly tucked under our mosquito net.

.....

We had to venture out on regular trips to unknown parts of the lake in search of crocodiles.

We travelled under a savage sun till dusk dimmed the harsh sunlight. Some way from shore multitudes of big hungry mosquitoes swarmed out to meet us attacking any part of uncovered skin. We poled as fast as possible to reach the bank, unloaded and pitched the net. We lit a few small fires from damp vegetation creating as much smoke as possible in an attempt to drive off the maddening insects.

Sitting in the smoke in the darkness, I cooked some eggs and made tea on the primus stove. I then rolled in under the net partly to get away from the mosquitoes but mainly because the heat of the day had exhausted me. I was blissfully unaware that we were camped only a few yards from a vast swamp.

I woke towards morning to find Jeff sitting, torch in hand, next to the bed.

"What's up?" I asked, alarmed.

"Look". He said playing the beam over the marsh.

Several pairs of red crocodile eyes glowed in the light. I leapt up, heart thudding.

"You should have woken me", I told Jeff looking into his pitifully tired face. We moved the bed close to the water's edge and slept for a few restless hours till dawn when once again mosquitoes had their fill of our blood.

.....

For fourteen sweltering days we traversed the great expanse of water setting off at first light each day, not turning the canoe shore-wards before the sun dipped away behind the horizon in gaudy splendour. I travelled with an inner tube about my hips, gun belt and Webley Colt strapped around my waist day and night, the primus stove lodged between my feet. The white bleached sky darkened, lightning tore into it, rain fell. We made no attempt to keep dry and revelled in the wet coolness on sunburned skin.

At night, we would retreat under our mosquito net and lying on the unyielding ground, would discuss the day's events till sleep overtook us.

One night we found ourselves at the foot of a gigantic sand dune with precious little level ground on which to camp. Sinking ankle deep into the sand, we lugged everything up to the top and made our bed under some sparse shrubbery.

Pale fingers of dawn had barely inched into the night blackness when all but inaudible whispering woke me. I peered from under slitted lids. Hovering close was a sea of black faces. In mortal fear I reached for the revolver on my hip and leapt from under the net firing a shot into the air.

The black youngsters fled en mass, scrambling screaming down the dune sending buckets and tins flying. Jeff tumbled from under the net.

"Don't ever" he panted "do that again".

Still dazed I mumbled" Okay" and sat down hard to recover my breath.

.....

The first rains came at midnight. A thunderous clap, electric white light flashing from one grass wall to the other, piercing through closed lids, shaking the earth, illuminating the entire hut. In a heartbeat the heavens opened her sluice gates releasing torrents of water that poured unhindered through the roof. Speechless, we leapt up, flung a tarpaulin over the net above our bed and stowed clothing cushions and blankets. In moments this was the only dry spot in the hut.

Jeff found his old police rain-cape, draped it over my shoulders, stuck a pith helmet on my head and slung a second cape over his own shoulders. That is how we sat on soaking deck chairs smoking Tom Tom cigarettes, water dripping from the peaks of our helmets.

Lightning continued tearing at the sky, thunder reverberated and rumbled noisily away then came roaring back over our heads, wind pushed through the thin walls. We sat in cold silence. Hours passed. Pools formed in the sand at our feet.

At last dawn crawled into sight and the storm grumbled slowly away, squeezing the last clouds dry. Unbeknown to us this was the time when the fish began moving into the tributaries to breed, severely affecting our food source.

"You," Jeff said never losing his sense of humour "look like the chief gnome in a rain forest".

Gingerly we dragged open the door to our abode. A shock awaited us. Thatch torn from the roof lay scattered about. The lake had risen dramatically and was lapping not two metres from where we stood.

"What will we do?" I asked feeling very small and frightened.

"Move house" Jeff said.

At sunrise, Nason was summoned and sent to the village to recruit labour which he promptly did. The entire structure was lifted, a new shallow foundation dug and the whole thing set up again by the end of the day. We were now perhaps sixty metres from the water's edge feeling very brave and safe.

.....

A solitary wave curled on the horizon, stole across the gilt edged water silent as a beast of prey, hit the canoe side on, rode in under it, lifted, held it quivering at its crest. We tilted precariously, roller-coasted back. An involuntary cry broke from my lips. Then all hell broke loose. Wind scurried in behind the wave, sucked up huge quantities of water, spewed it into our faces splashing around our feet. Blind in the frenzied darkness, deafened by the now insanely roaring lake I clung to the sides of the canoe, only one coherent thought thumping in my brain. I could not swim. If we capsized how long would I flounder before a crocodile took me below and stashed my body under a rock?

Nason at the prow panicked and released his pole. He started to wail with fear. Jeff, legs splayed, grabbed the pole as it toppled, plunged it back into the water. He and Mulenga fought the storm, frantically trying to guide the little craft shorewards.

After what seemed an eternity Mulenga cried out above the wind, his free arm motioning. I plucked the hair from my eyes. A tattered cloud covered the yellow moon. Ahead a grove of reeds, swaying ghostlike, beckoned. The two men pushed with all their might. This was a lifeline. It had to be reached.

The canoe inched forward, closer to the relative calm afforded by the quavering reeds until our outstretched hands reached them. Nason had risen, the wailing stilled. Grabbing convulsively we heaved until the reeds folded about us.

"Take the pole" Jeff shouted.

I collapsed into his arms, felt the wild beating of his heart through his sodden shirt. The storm raged on. We clung together, seeking what comfort we could from the meagre warmth of each other's bodies. Moments later Jeff let me go, retrieved the pole, tested the water's depth.

"Too deep for you to wade," he said "I'll have to piggy-back you." I climbed onto his back, rifles swinging from my shoulders. He surged along parting the growth as he went. We reached our refuge. Jeff fumbled for the torch he'd dropped down his shirt front, flicked it on. In its feeble light appeared a raised dune no bigger than a small room. The moon had crept from behind the obscuring cloud, an immense lamp in the ebony sky. A frog croaked cautiously. A bird twittered briefly. Jeff lowered me onto the damp sand, sat down beside me. The two black men exchanged monosyllables in hushed tones and fell silent. Shoulders touching the four of us waited for the new day.

In the pre-dawn chill I raised my head. The lake lay spent under a mother of pearl dome. Gradually a pink flush suffused the sky. Emboldened birds rose from their night perches. Mosquitoes heavy with our blood drifted sluggishly away.

The men waded to where the canoe rocked among the reeds, dragged its nose onto the sand. It was more than half filled with sand and water. We buried our hands in the soggy mess, lifted out boxes, bedding and the precious primus stove. We spread out the blankets on the reeds and laid out everything we could salvage, then set about bailing the water out with saucepan, mugs and cupped hands. The sun was hot and blazing orange by the time we completed the task.

Jeff cleaned and oiled the rifles. I smoked damp cigarettes, my stomach gnawing. A breeze sprung up cooling my cheeks, rustling the reeds. Jeff glanced skywards, amber eyes glowing.

"I'm going to rig up a sail and see what's around the bend."

"You're what?" I choked.

"Can't stay here another night. We must find food" he replied grabbing the biggest blanket.

I lay on my back. The sun stung my lids. After a while tears of exhaustion overflowed and ran down into my ears. Would this nightmare never end? Would I be hungry and frightened forever?

"Look" Jeff called "it's ready".

I blinked back the tears. He had transformed the humble blanket with astonishing ingenuity, into a vigorously flapping sail, a schoolboy grin superimposed over the tired lines on his face.

I reluctantly agreed to remain on the dune whilst the men went forth with cheery shouts, waving until the canoe vanished from sight. I slumped down amongst our pitiful belongings and wrapped myself in a still damp blanket.

Endless grey water, my impregnable prison from which there was no escape, lapped to the horizon. I sobbed, felt for the Webley Colt strapped around my hips, clung to the stock of the.22 Jeff had left with me. An overwhelming fear crept into my bones, my gums tingled, my scalp crawled, my trembling hands turned to ice. The half formed thought I'd been trying to suppress grew in stature. What if the canoe capsized and not one of the three occupants survived. The horrendous reality was that they alone knew where I was. I would starve to death, the lake would rise in black terror and sweep me away like some pale infinitesimal flotsam.

"No!" I said aloud pushing the vision from my mind. I stared at the sky, made pictures of the cloud formations, tried to guess what bird had winged overhead, drew in the sand with a stick and watched the water till my eyes burned. The sun was close to the horizon burnishing the emptiness in spectacular orange and cerise, when the dugout, its makeshift sail ballooning in the breeze, came into view. Waving in wild joy I dashed ankle deep into the water as the men got out, wrapped my arms around my beloved Jeff and burst into tears.

"Perfect" Jeff said, bright eyed with enthusiasm, "we found the perfect spot".

Eager to get away, dry land and food beckoning, we quickly loaded the canoe, sailed across the now docile water, rounded a corner and there sure enough was paradise. A curve of snow white beach, clumps of trees, thatch roofs visible above the scant vegetation.

"Looks wonderful" I said shielding my eyes.

"Told you" Jeff grinned.

Little could we guess that by nightfall we'd be virtual castaways in this deceptive Shangrila.

We unpacked, gave the fishermen some money.

"Buy food" Jeff told them "anything you can find".

We donned swimsuits, washed ourselves, played about in the sparkling water. Still damp we gathered kindling, blew a small fire into life, made tea and waited. The sun rolled away. Night fell.

Still no sign of the polers. Our earlier high spirits were dwindling. Stomachs gnawing we sat in silence.

"Missies" a voice startled us.

"Who's there?" Jeff growled, rising.

A pale brown face peeped from behind a tree, a hand held out a rusty tin.

"Mealie meal for you" said the voice

"Who are you?" I asked taking the tin.

"I James from South Africa".

"Where are our men?" Jeff asked

"They take your money. They afraid. They say too much storm. People drown. They run away." he replied, still partly obscured behind the tree.

"Hell" Jeff exclaimed "you mean...?"

71

But he'd vanished as mysteriously as he'd arrived. Slowly, painfully the truth dawned. We'd been abandoned. Left helpless, stranded.

Tired and despondent after a sleepless night Jeff suggested we go into the village, firstly to find out if our mysterious visitor of the previous night had indeed given us the correct story regarding the bearers and more importantly, to find food.

We wandered in among the huts, children, chickens and dogs scattering.

"Have you seen my men Nason and Mulenga?" Jeff asked a woman.

"Don't know. Ask the men", she said stirring a huge iron pot.

We approached a man repairing a net in the doorway of his hut.

"No" he said averting his dark eyes.

"Can you sell us something to eat, eggs, rice, anything?"

"Nothing" he replied, again dropping his lids" we have nothing", he rose bent his head and went into his hut.

After an hour of unanswered questions we returned to camp totally dejected, empty handed.

We prepared our rods, baited our hooks and fished for endless hours, first one spot then another with not a single bite as reward. By evening, ravenously hungry, we brewed the last of our tea and cooked the remaining handful of bitter, gritty meal.

We tossed and turned on the hard ground, sat up before dawn, made a fire. At sunrise took the rods, some bait and the binoculars and strolled down the beach.

"Lot of croc sunbathing over there" Jeff said focussing on a large spit of sand that jutted out into the lake.

"Let's go and see".

We walked in a huge half circle to reach it. As we approached several large crocodile slipped into the water. We cast our rods but again caught nothing.

Weak with hunger, each silently wondering how we were going to get away, and why the local people were so withdrawn and unfriendly. Where were we going to find willing fishermen to take us the rest of the way? We slowly made our way back.

Late afternoon with the binoculars to his eyes, Jeff suddenly exclaimed

"People!"

"People?" I repeated stupidly

"On the spit" he said "I think they're Europeans".

I grabbed the binoculars. Two white men and a woman were clearly visible. We waved, shouting as we ran for the canoe and jumped aboard. Please God I prayed, let them see us. Don't let them go away. I thrust my pole into the water, wobbled. Unable to synchronise our strokes we literally rocked our way the short distance shouting all the while.

The three on the spit crowded close to the water's edge gaping in astonishment as we approached.

"Good grief" the younger of the men exclaimed as Jeff jumped ashore. "Where did you come from?"

"You might well ask" Jeff grinned holding out his hand introducing himself.

"And this is my wife" he said an arm around my shoulders.

"Name's Allen" the young man said "Gail and Bert" he waved a hand towards the couple still staring at us in disbelief.

Amid much chatter they explained that they were civil servants teaching the local people how to grow tobacco and that they called around every three months to check on progress and to give further instructions.

"What brought you to the spit?" I asked Gail, amazed at what was surely a miracle of chance.

"Cook" the girl said," you know how fast news travels in the bush".

I did know. Silently I thanked Providence for the fleetness of bare black feet and the voice of the drums.

We beached our canoe, walked back to camp where our new-found friends helped us pack.

"Our camp's not far from here. Spend the night. Patel, he has a store down the road. He comes past every other day on his way to Salima. You can catch a lift with him" Allen said.

Their camp turned out to be a large, comfortable tent. We feasted on tinned beans, bacon, tinned fruit and coffee. At around ten am next morning Mr. Patel's lorry came into view. Allen flagged him down. He willingly agreed to give us a lift.

"Glad to have company" he smiled.

We clambered on, thanked and bade our friends good-bye and set off on a bumpy ride to Salima.

.....

We were ignorant and fearless and did some very silly things, often not realising how dangerous our situation was. Our outboard motor caused endless trouble so we relied on a dugout canoe and two men to pole us around the lake as we hunted crocodiles. I felt quite sick seeing them being skinned. On one occasion Jeff and I ended up having to carry a wet croc skin slung over a pole. The huge difference in our heights meant that the skin kept slipping down to my end making it unbearably heavy. We had to stop every five paces to re-adjust the weight.

With all the rain, our forty odd hides began to rot in the damp. They were stored in a simple hut that leaked. Time was running out. Our six month license was almost up. With heavy hearts we started planning our return.

We were broke, carless, homeless, sunburned, bleached and a huge failure. Our plan was to reach the nearest railhead about eighty miles away and get a train back to Blantyre from there. We sold what we could to the Indian shopkeeper for £25. Jeff patched up the leaking boat and loaded our few possessions into it. After a mile or so the outboard gave up and we had to return to our base. We slept on the bare sand and in the morning arranged for the old twenty four foot dugout and two polers to collect us.

With a few bananas, a little tea and sugar and some tinned food, we began our journey back to civilisation.

The Great Jail Breaker

Compiled from original sources, magazine articles, news features and as much other material as became available, by Peter Dearlove.

Aiden Diggeden. Two words, five syllables to make the heart beat faster for all who lived in Rhodesia over one weird decade last century when a man of that name made crime seem exciting and almost respectable. From one end of the country to the other the Rhodesian public watched in fascination as an engaging petty crook made his way into legend and the history books with robberies, breakouts, and bravado.

His life was the wildest soap opera of them all.

Aiden's story as it has come down to us is a story only of his duel with the law, and the attached incidents that made him famous. Little is known about his private life, if he had one. Love, marriage, children – all seem to be parts of the human journey that eluded him. Yet he lived to be about 70, a playful, confident, and non-violent villain who never made much of a living from of his extraordinary fame.

By accepted accounts Diggeden was born in about 1940 and was adopted by a family living in what was then Gwelo, Southern Rhodesia. He went to Chaplin School in that town, or so they say – no one so far has been able to retrieve any school reports to certify the fact. Nor are there any clues as to his young character. It was only once he had moved to the other side of the

77

law that people began to put the two's together and say confidingly that they always knew he was a 'wrong one'.

One woman who claimed to have known Aiden as a youngster said years later that he had drifted into a life of crime because his parents could not afford to give him anything like the customary small allowance of pocket money.

Whatever may be the truth of that, he certainly began his criminal career quite young. In Gwelo he broke into shops and stole a car, but was quickly caught and sent to prison in the city of Bulawayo. Detectives who worked on his many cases over the years were unanimous in declaring him a quick and novel thinker but pretty useless at his chosen trade.

What he did prove to have an incredible talent for, however, was lateral thought and... escape.

His first demonstration of the ability to think sideways was when he was in prison that first time. It was in the early sixties, and he was in for his original sins of stealing a car and breaking into a store. He and a couple of other enterprising inmates cooked up what they thought would be a fool-proof scheme to make on-going crime pay – they would steal the city blind while safely locked up in prison. There could be no better alibi than to be able to say "couldn't possibly have been me Sir, I was locked up at the time, don't you remember?"

The way to make that scheme a reality, they decided, was to do a deal, so they put it to a guard who seemed friendly. In return for letting them out of prison at night and then back in a few hours later, he would get a fair slice of the pie.

Bingo! The lure of gold did the trick.

No one now remembers how long this first scam went on, but it certainly worked out on a number of occasions over a period of a month or more.

How they were eventually caught had to do with Aiden's taste in motor cars. He loved Fords. It wasn't that he'd ever legitimately owned one, or that he thought them the best cars under the sun; it was just that he knew how to hot-wire a Ford and get it going without keys. To get back to prison with the loot from their night's work the three of them would steal a Ford and head back 'home', leaving the stolen car within easy walk of the prison gates. That behaviour, plus the fact that some of the hot property was actually found within the prison itself, was what did for Diggeden that first time.

Under tough questioning his associates were first to crack, but he too eventually admitted the scam. It meant court again; another trial, and the prospect of extra time inside. That was something he did not fancy, and he quickly set about a plan to get out for good. It was quite a complicated idea, but it worked for him. Somehow he persuaded a number of fellow prison inmates to stage a mass break-out on a particular day. The scheme went ahead, and in the confusion Aiden made good his departure, but he was the only one – all the rest were quickly put back in their pens.

This was actually his first escape, and as it turned out, probably his most successful, if not most spectacular. He was on the run for nearly three years, most of that time in South Africa where he gave himself a new name, achieved a surprising degree of athletic fame, and continued to steal cars – Fords for preference.

He called himself Colin Nicholas Truter. Where he got the name from no one knows, but he used it for a few years as a car salesman and once as a 'financial manager' for a firm in Cape Town. It was in the offices of that company that the police finally arrived to arrest him. He was charged with many miscellaneous offences, but broke bail and bolted.

In the meantime Aiden had become a trampoline champion. Always something of a fitness fanatic, he liked jumping up and down, and he developed amazing skills on the trampoline – so amazing that he won prizes and titles. This may be an exaggeration – once again no one has been able to dig up proof of his wins or titles. All they can say for sure is that he was a bit of a gymnast – as we will later find out from one of his subsequent prison adventures.

So he is on the run again. This time from the South African police who want him for a number of car thefts *and* jumping bail. By the skin of his teeth he gets away and arrives back in Rhodesia in early 1966 with a man by the name of Dilman, who sounds a bit like the American gangster Dillinger by the way, travelling by car and clearing the border as 'in transit' visitors, at Forbes

Border Post, Umtali, on the Rhodesian border with Mozambique. They are on their way to Zambia.

Needing money, they stopped over for a while in Salisbury, and immediately robbed a building society office in the little suburb of Mabelreign. The teller found herself staring at the barrel of a gun, so she handed over all she could, a fair sum in those days, almost two thousand dollars. The pair then headed off to Bulawayo in a stolen car, this time a Mini Cooper, a rare enough super model to turn heads even then. This is where it is easy to accept the view of people who thought Aiden 'a bit thick', for how he hoped to evade attention in that hot little number is difficult to comprehend. And indeed it was not long before the police traced the car, and he and Dilman, to a hotel in Bulawayo. They were enjoying a full English breakfast at the moment the law arrived, but, sitting on the hotel veranda they could see the police cars screeching towards the hotel from a distance. Without waiting to find out who the police were after, they dashed off to find another car, leaving the Cooper in its parking spot, and most of the stolen money in their room. The entire hotel was soon fairly abuzz with armed police, but of Diggeden and his mate there was no trace.

Despite a nationwide manhunt it quickly became apparent that the two had vanished. Actually they were in Zambia, but how he got there, or across which border, is not known. The passports they had used to get into Rhodesia had been left behind with the bulk of the loot in the Bulawayo hotel bedroom.

81

Smart detectives scratched their heads. But not for long. They knew Diggeden would surface again sooner or later. It turned out to be sooner rather than later. Within weeks he had been arrested in Zambia for car theft. He was sentenced to three years in jail.

All of this was going on less than a year after Rhodesia had declared itself 'independent', and the relationship between that country and Zambia was under some strain. Nonetheless, the Rhodesian authorities had applied for the extradition of the two robbers, and Rhodesian detectives travelled to Zambia to interview them.

Diggeden was due in court in Lusaka the next day to answer charges that he had conspired to escape, but the interrogation session went ahead as planned and he was advised that as soon as his Zambian term was over he would be extradited to Rhodesia to face an armed robbery charge arising from the Mabelreign caper.

It was a relaxed and easy conversation in which Diggeden admitted his part in the Mabelreign case, but assured his questioners that he had never gone in for violence, and the 'gun' had been a plastic toy.

Then the ever-confident bank robber asked them when they were planning to go home. When they told him they would be leaving the next day he jokingly wagered that he would be back in Rhodesia before them.

Roy Welsh, who was one of those policemen, recorded the event later in an article for the police magazine Outpost.

"At the conclusion of proceedings in the Lusaka Magistrates court, Diggeden, who was unguarded and untethered, walked slowly from the dock to an open and unguarded door leading through a short passageway to the main entrance to the court building – he most certainly did not jump up and run out of the court as some reports have stated."

While they watched, they had no idea that Diggeden's casual departure was an escape.

"We had in fact warned the Zambians that Aiden would try something, but they politely told us to leave prisoner security to them.

"It was only the day after we arrived back at our offices in Salisbury that we found out for certain he had escaped, and by that time he was already in Bulawayo, having got there on the overnight train."

His freedom was short, however, and he was arrested in Bulawayo within days. In court he pleaded guilty to the many charges against him and was sentenced to thirteen years.

In a way, that sentence marks the beginning of Diggeden's real 'glory' days. With it began a long series of break-out and capture that kept the Rhodesian public agog for years. His name was on everybody's lips. People who were children then still remember how their parents seemed to wish him well and how they secretly egged him on to the next dramatic instalment.

"Go Aiden, Go!" was the popular response to every new headline the man made.

That growing public reputation and admiration persuaded the authorities to transfer him to Salisbury's maximum security prison· at an out-of-town place called Chikurubi. But less than a year later he pulled off what was described at the time as the most daring and ingenious escape in the annals of Rhodesian justice.

The story goes that he had 'by chance' come across the key to the maximum security wing.

By chance my foot. Now, almost forty years after these events, it is surely obvious that, being the man he was, Aiden bribed his way to a moment alone with the key. In any case he had his moment with the key, and he quickly sketched its 'key' features. Later he made a copy of it in the prison workshop where he was employed much of the time. He also made a key to the more accessible loft in the high security section.

The plan was that he and a fellow inmate, Lionel Barker, would make their way in the dead of night up to the loft, and from there to an opening overlooking a less secure part of the prison premises. They had stashed enough stolen towels and sheets to make a kind of rope ladder that would let them down the thirty odd feet to the ground. Diggeden managed the drop without a problem, but beefy Barker was too heavy for the ladder, and it broke, sending him to guaranteed injury below.

To his credit Diggeden refused to abandon Barker, and he carried him to the prison Chapel where he made him as comfortable as he could, staying with him until almost first light. Then he took a chapel bench out to the wall and used it to get over the top. Next he walked off to the prison parking area and in the half light of dawn picked out one of the trucks known to be used regularly for trips to town. Waiting for the first signs of movement, he squeezed his way into position between the chassis and the main body. At 5.30 the truck was driven out of the prison gates and he was on the loose. But the vehicle was only going somewhere within the general prison grounds and he had to find some other means to make good the escape. He stole a policeman's bicycle, and rode into the city, a free man once more.

Making his devil-may-care way to his favourite city of Bulawayo, he again left behind a trail of stolen Fords, so the police knew exactly where to look for him. Once again they only had to bide their time. On February 7th 1967 a storekeeper telephoned the police to report that a man who might have been Diggeden had been in the store and had then boarded a bus bound for Essexvale.

He was quickly picked up at a road block and taken back to Salisbury where he was soon in court again and sentenced to another lengthy period in jail.

You would think he had had enough.

But uh-uh. He made two more serious attempts, both of them worthy of his now world-wide reputation as the Rhodesian Houdini, Master of the Prison Break Out.

About a year after his recapture he asked to see a prison official to make a complaint in person. Marching back to the cells after a brief interview he seized the chance to bolt, sprinting past his surprised guards and scaling, so they say, a sixteen-foot wall – testament, perhaps, to his championship trampoline days. But he was easily caught on the other side and nothing more came of that particular episode except a slap on the wrists by way of yet another addition to his sentence.

In August that year he tried his luck once more. It was thought he had succeeded, for he simply disappeared and was nowhere to be found. But then, after a day or two 'away' he was found hiding in a water tank, up to his nose in water, among the rafters above his high security cell, only waiting till the hue and cry died down before his next step.

Another slap on the wrists.

He was now looking at 17 years inside. It was a prospect too heavy to handle and so he tried once more to get away, this time with two other inmates.

Diggeden dressed himself up as a prison guard in gear he had stolen for the occasion, and he and the other two marched about the yard as if on a regular prison mission – ostensibly with him in charge of the small party. The two others were carrying a film projector and screen which they had liberated for the moment. At the main gate Diggeden managed to disguise his voice and put on an air of authority. He said to the guard that he was taking the 'gang' to the warder's mess where they were to show a film.

Incredibly, the duty officer let them out, and once again a trail of stolen Ford's helped the law to find them.

Yet another slap on the wrists – another two years hard labour. This time, however, the slap proved to be terminal – never again did Diggeden try to get out.

He served twelve years of a sentence of eighteen years and was released from prison on 16 November 1978.

By then he had decided he needed to go where he was less well-known. Within days of leaving prison he left the country for England, taking with him at least a thousand pounds he had earned while in prison in a curious but typical Diggeden way. Some have accused him of turning police informer, but there is no evidence of a real sea change of that sort. What happened was that he came into possession of information he knew the police would pay for. He offered it to them at a price, and they accepted. Ask Roy Welsh.

Here's the way it was.

In April of 1978 while Diggeden was still safely locked up and now quietly serving his time, a man called Berwick James ambushed and murdered two colleagues from the Arcturus mine near Salisbury to steal the substantial payroll cash they were carrying. He used an AK 47 communist rifle, hoping to make the crime look like a terrorist hit. The police quickly solved the case, however, and James was sentenced to death, despite the fact that the murder weapon had not been found. From bullets and bullet holes they had surmised that the weapon was a sawn-off AK, which in the end it did prove to be.

Still in jail at the time, Aiden befriended the man awaiting hanging, and they became quite close. Close enough anyway, for Berwick to confide in him where he had hidden the murder weapon.

Spotting the opportunity, Aiden contacted the police and offered them the information for £500 up front, and another £500 if it led to the recovery of the rifle.

It did. They found the sawn-off AK in a roadside culvert exactly where Aiden had described. He got his reward money and it made no difference to James. Due to be hanged for his crime, he managed to get a razor blade into his cell and with it he ended his own life.

When Aiden was let out a few weeks later at least he had a little 'seed' capital.

Unfortunately it was not enough, for although he got a respectable start in the UK, it was not long before he worked out an elaborate plan to steal money from his employer. It was a complicated and quite intelligent scam involving the opening of a bank account very similar in name to that of the business. And he might easily have got away with it, but this time his body let him down, or so he said.

In mitigation he told the court that he used the money to invest in South African gold coins – Kruger Rands – and that he all along intended to return it as soon as he had made a profit. Unfortunately his time was cut short when he had to be rushed to hospital for a burst appendix. While there, the theft was uncovered. He was sent to jail once more.

There is no record of any attempted break out in Great Britain. He served his time and left the UK.

Aiden died in 2014, or so it was put out. No one seems to know for sure.

Of a heart attack in the Zimbabwe capital, Harare, formerly Salisbury and scene of many of his most exciting years. Maybe.

Or somewhere else.

Living under another name. And only identified, fittingly, at *post mortem,* by his fingerprints.

Flash Flood
Brian Sherry

The northern part of Gonarezhou National Park is bisected by the Runde River, which, together with the Chilojo sandstone cliffs, forms an impressive and pristine centre-piece for this fantastic part of the Lowveld. The river rises over 200 km away to the north-west, up towards the central watershed, and where it enters the park it is one of the country's largest 'sand' rivers – up to a couple of hundred metres wide. At Chipinda Pools, the headquarters for the northern part of the park, it narrows and plunges over the Selawandoma Falls as it gouges its way through the rugged Chuanja Hills. From here it is restricted for many miles by a narrow gorge through the granitic rock before spilling out at the mouth into Chinguli Pool; once again to become a wide, relatively slow-flowing 'sand' river down to the Sabi on the border with Mozambique.

One of my roles as Wildlife Research Officer (Ecologist) in that beautiful park from 1969 to 1977 was to monitor changes in vegetation, especially in some of the more sensitive areas. This involved setting up sturdily-fenced exclosure plots to provide protection from the depredations of larger herbivores such as elephant and hippo. Measuring vegetation every few years both within and outside these exclosures would help us to keep an objective eye on habitat changes over the years.

In January 1971 we put in the first of these plots in the northern part of the park. It was quite an undertaking, involving the construction of a robust 2-metre-high game fence around a 50 metre square, with a wide, steep-sided waist-deep trench all the way around to keep elephants out.

At this time of the year the Runde was impassable to vehicles, and access to the south of the river was by boat at Chipinda Pools. We kept a Land Rover on the south bank there for patrol work into that part of the park. We used this Landie to ferry ourselves, our kit and the tools and equipment down to the Fishans area, about 30 miles away. Myself and Angus Anthony, the Research Ranger, with Lukas the Research Scout and a small gang of labourers established a camp at Linanga; a point between Chinguli Pool at the mouth of the Runde Gorge and Fishans. With us was Ian Mullen, a volunteer student who was there for field experience. The steep north bank of the river at this point, bounded by a narrow, sparsely treed alluvial plain, breaks down into a mixed series of lower banks, mud-banks and sand bars with scattered reed-beds, before levelling off into the relatively flat sandy river bed, through which the actual river channel meanders during the dry season. We set up camp under a fine clump of riverine trees on the high south bank, which provided a commanding view of the river, upstream to Chinguli Pool and the mouth of the gorge, and downstream to the Fishans alluvium and the Chilojo Cliffs.

Once the task was well under way I returned to Chipinda Pools for a few days, to take the Land Rover back and attend a meeting. I then returned in my own Land Rover, with a canoe on top. On arrival at Linanga, I drove down into the river bed, leaving the vehicle parked on a grassy sand bank a little way from the main river channel. It was a straightforward task to unload the one-man kayak, drag it across the sand to the water's edge and paddle across the relatively calm 2-metre deep river little more than 50 metres wide in the main channel. I pulled the canoe up onto high ground near our camp and joined the gang working on our exclosure plot for the rest of the day.

Being well into the rainy season it was oppressively hot and humid, and we'd been seeing flashes of lightning at night on the far horizon upstream for a few days before, so we knew there had been thunder storms and rain many miles away up towards the central watershed. As we sat relaxing and cooling off at the end of a long day, overlooking a large rocky pool full of hippos while the odd herd of elephants and various antelope came to drink downstream, we noticed a kind of restlessness amongst the 30-odd hippos, and we soon grasped that the river was rising rather rapidly. The hippos' vocalisation intensified and as the water continued to rise they began to leave the pool and move off slowly down stream.

This clearly was the beginnings of a flash flood. With my Land Rover parked close to the edge of the river's sandy bed on the far side, and the water rapidly rising I realised that the vehicle was in danger of being submerged or washed away. I had to act quickly. The evening light was beginning to fade.

Picking up the vehicle keys and strapping my heavy 45 Colt revolver to my waist I was soon in the canoe, paddling urgently across the now few hundred metres of river. The crossing was no problem although I was a little uneasy to find myself in amongst some of the hippos moving downstream; one spurred me on to paddle a little deeper and with more purpose as it approached wide-eyed, meaningfully and menacingly in mid-stream.

Having been carried more than 100 metres downstream by the floodwater, I beached the canoe, dragging it up onto a sand bar well above the rising water. Then I hurried upstream on foot to the Land Rover, by now only a few metres clear of the water. Within minutes I had driven it up into a secure position high above the rising water level on a raised part of the main alluvial plain, and was ready to return.

The river meanwhile had risen substantially, the water now swirling and eddying angrily, already covering the spot where the Land Rover had stood only minutes before, and lapping the tail end of the canoe. Getting to it as quickly as I could I dragged it through shallow water upstream to a point beyond where the Land Rover had been parked, and prepared for the crossing.

The river had risen nearly three metres, and was already 150 metres wide, and the current appeared to have increased at least five-fold. Most of the hippos from the school in the pool above our camp had drifted downstream, and now were spread out haphazardly across my path, so to get back I was going to have to run the gauntlet under somewhat tricky conditions. The dark water was swirling in great eddies, right across the river width; making swells and low waves in parts. A few logs and other bits of flotsam and foam rounded out the picture. In the rapidly fading evening light hippos were my main concern and I didn't give crocodiles a thought.

Still in the shallows I hauled the nose of the canoe round to point upstream, lowered myself aboard and paddled tentatively and obliquely out amongst the sand bars and reed-beds, trying to use these as a protective guide into the main channel of the river. As I prepared to launch away from the shelter of one of these semi-submerged islands I ran onto something solid and hard. I thought it was a log. But suddenly the log exploded into life in the form of a large crocodile. It must have been sheltering from the rising water and it probably got as much of a fright as I did. It thrashed about wildly in the shallows in its escape from under me, nearly capsizing me in the process. In reaction I in turn thrashed about with my paddle and desperately propelled the wobbling canoe into the main stream of the river, at right angles to the current, instead of keeping the nose pointing upstream. In my frantic attempt to distance myself from the croc, I dug in so deep on the upstream side that the upstream deck went under, and the current did the rest.

It's an eerie and scary feeling to be upended in the dusk in a wide, powerful, murky river, full of restless hippos and who knows how many restless crocodiles. Needless to say, I parted company with the canoe and sank from underneath it, still hanging on with one hand to the paddle; conscious that my revolver, strapped into its holster on my belt, was of absolutely no use to me under these conditions. In fact, it was more of a hindrance – the hefty Colt was now a diver's weight-belt.

I came spluttering to the surface to see the canoe sweeping away from me, out towards mid-stream. I couldn't swim effectively with the paddle, but seeing the canoe now drifting back towards the bank, I let go of the paddle and swam furiously to intercept the canoe. Having caught up with it I now watched the paddle drifting by, just out of reach. I swung the nose of the canoe towards the shore and gave it a mighty heave – it was upside down, pretty near full of water and felt as heavy as one of the several hippos watching all the goings-on from close quarters – and it drifted unwillingly in the direction of the river bank. Then I swam furiously after the paddle and thankfully caught up with it, now slightly ahead of the canoe!

With a bit of fancy treading water *cum* swimming, and still hanging onto the paddle, I intercepted the canoe and hung on with relief. It wasn't long before I had angled towards the bank sufficiently to be able to touch bottom with my feet, and steer into the bank, some hundreds of metres downstream from my starting point. But I had ended up on the wrong side of the river!

95

It's a somewhat frightening and humbling experience to feel so deeply immersed and floundering in the water when your instinct tells you that you should be *walking* around it, out of the way of ponderous hippos and lurking crocodiles!

With considerable relief I hauled the canoe out onto the river bank, the adrenalin rush allowing me to make relatively light work of this. Righting the cumbersome beast and emptying it of water was another story, and I was pretty well exhausted by the time I was ready to try the crossing again. Now for a second attempt.

Where I now was I didn't have the 'luxury' of sand bars, nor, any longer, much light!

Once again I dragged the canoe a few hundred metres upstream through the shallows, before getting in and paddling very carefully upstream. This time, while still in the shallows, I made sure to angle the bow upstream, and then paddled with furious determination back to safety; under the watchful eyes of a few nearby hippo. Eventually, as the evening closed in, I reached the far bank, a few hundred metres downstream from camp.

I was *really* knackered as I hauled the canoe up onto the high river bank and walked slowly to the camp. It was nigh on dark by now and Angus, Ian and the Scouts were hardly even aware of the difficulties I had got myself into.

What a relief to change into dry clothes and to sit and recover beside the camp fire, the companionship of camp-mates contrasting strongly with the feeling of sheer loneliness and fear out there in the deep dark water.

Not much of an appetite that night, and very early to bed.

By Kayak to the Sea.

In Three parts.
Ralph Stutchbury.

In 1995 I was asked by Larry Norton to take over the filming of his adventurous journey from the source of the Zambezi, to the sea. For various reasons his original camera operator was not able to complete the final third of the project through Mozambique to Chinde and the ocean. I snapped at the offer, it was much too good to turn down.

Larry had arranged for people to help us along the way. The first was Pete Hougaard who had a hunting concession on the Zambezi in Mozambique. It was his supply vehicle which took us on the first leg. Oskar Komen and Steve Johnson were two young friends of Larry's who took us the length of Cabora Basa in their speedboat.

We later met up with four adventurers with their own kayaks and provisions, in Tete. Mike Stewart was an ocean competition kayaker whose experience was essential for the final leg up the coast. Alistair Stobart and Paul Dawson were also fit, experienced kayakers with military experience. They were along for the challenge and to make up a team capable of dealing with a potentially dangerous and arduous journey.

98

I was older than the others, unfit, and with no kayaking experience. To make matters worse, I suffer from motion sickness.

Part 1

Mvurwi to Caia

For me the journey began in Mvurwi, a small farming village in Zimbabwe. From there Larry, who had broken his trip to find a replacement cameraman, and I had to get to the Zambezi.

At 4am in the morning of August 5, 1995, we waited in the dark outside the service station with our personal gear and a mountain of video and photographic equipment. We wondered what the coming weeks would hold for us. After a rather solid cold pork pie, our lift arrived and we set off into the first glow of dawn, glad to be on our way. The winter morning was bitterly cold. We put on balaclavas, wrapped ourselves in our sleeping bags, and lay, still cold and a little nervous, on the back of the over-laden land cruiser as it lurched and swayed its way north. We thought this was probably going to be the most perilous part of the journey.

Granite domes rose from the fields and the grass glowed gold in the early morning sunlight. If it weren't for the ominous swaying of the vehicle it would have been idyllic. Each time our driver moved over to avoid oncoming buses, the drop off the tarmac threatened to capsize us.

At Guruve we thankfully changed vehicles. Commercial farmland gave way to communal land with small clusters of African huts amidst the dry open ploughed lands. In the distance the great dyke receded and the road narrowed. Around 9am we reached the Zambezi escarpment and began a winding descent through the foothills. Dotted all around were small clusters of huts and recently cleared fields of new settlers. People had settled illegally and randomly on the hillsides, clearing and burning to create fields for their crops of maize. When the rain comes, what little topsoil there is will almost certainly erode and wash away into the valley below.

At the bottom of the escarpment the tar ended and the corrugations and dust began. The gravel road continued north through the communal lands with baobabs now dotted about.

At the small settlement of Mushumbi Pools we drank cold drinks and waited in the heat outside a rural trader's shop as people came to grind their maize at the noisy hammer mill. Here a second support vehicle caught up and we drove off together into the very sparsely populated area of wild country that continues all the way to Kanyemba, the most North Easterly village in Zimbabwe. This is the border post where the three countries. Zimbabwe, Zambia and Mozambique meet. Because of the low volume of traffic, there are no customs or immigration offices but an admin centre at the police camp where these formalities are dealt with. From Kanyemba we retraced our route for a few kilometres before turning off onto an obscure track that was to lead us into Mozambique. The track was rough and strewn with boulders as it led back down to the Zambezi River's edge through riverine forest.

The road ended in a small Mozambican village of huts opposite the border town of Zumbo. We had to send a man to track down the border officials who operate from a rickety mud hut next to the river Flies buzzed in the heat and village dogs stretched lazily in the shade as the children gathered round to gawk at our two vehicles laden with supplies and equipment for Pete Hougaard's hunting camp. Two surly men eventually appeared and set about searching through the contents of the vehicles. Larry and I were then dispatched across the river to Zumbo to complete the passport formalities.

Our guide was a bright young Mozambican from the recently formed Parks and Wildlife Department. The little speed boat sped across the wide sprawling river to land somewhat dangerously near dugout canoes and women washing clothes on the bank, our wake almost swamping us in the process. We walked up through scattered huts and men lounging about sheltering from the heat in search of the relevant official, but it was siesta time in Mozambique and so nothing would be done till at least 3pm. This civilised continental habit held us up for another hour. We wandered about the derelict remains of the old Portuguese town; rusting street lamps led along dusty tracks where streets had once been; avenues of trees along the remains of paved roads; once quite grand buildings decaying and unused, many without roofs.

We waited under a sprawling fig tree.

The immigration man finally appeared but had to go back for keys before letting us into a large dirty room. The dirt stained walls and peeling paint were broken here and there with dog eared Frelimo posters and nutrition information. The very skinny young man then painfully recorded the details from five passports into a ledger and took a $40 dollar fee for each. A queue of Zambian fish traders gathered behind us and waited patiently for their turn.

The 30-odd km drive along the floodplain to Hougaard's hunting camp on the river was a delight in the late afternoon. The road ran parallel to the river, passing now and again through small fishing villages before winding its way into deep riverine woodland. The area was spectacular and well stocked with game (but sadly, no elephant).

Pete's camp blends unobtrusively into the surrounding bush and looks out over the river on to three distinct blue grey mountains at the horizon. Each mountain is in a different country.

Pete took us out onto the river at sunset when the water glowed red from the reflections. We drank cool beers and watched the terrible battle for territory and mating rights between two massive bull hippos, their huge tusks inflicting bloody gashes in each other's necks and shoulders as they lunged noisily to the surface in this timeless struggle. Along the extensive reed-banks we saw slipways of nesting crocodiles and signs of where the eggs had been buried beneath the sand. Back at camp we showered under buckets of warm water drawn to the perfect temperature in the balmy evening. Dinner was tender buffalo fillet with piri piri and garlic sauce. We drank red wine and talked till we were too tired to speak any more, and collapsed into comfortable beds in our reed chalet. It was a great way to start our journey.

In the morning Larry painted the distant hills and the river from camp, his watercolours perfectly capturing the ambiance of this rarely seen part of the Zambezi. A few hours later after a hearty breakfast, we met Steve Johnson and Oskar Komen on a sand bar a few hundred metres upstream. We had canoed out to find them, knowing that the camp was hard to see from the water. They had travelled by boat 250km down the length of Cabora Bassa to collect us and take us on the next leg of our journey.

The boat was an 18ft Falcon with a 130 HP Yamaha motor that would speed us along at almost 60km/hr. While Steve and Oskar refuelled, Larry and I walked up to one of the larger villages, making our way through very unhealthy looking shallows between the reeds to get there, but it was deserted except for a few raggedy children, goats chickens and a pig. So we made our way back to the boat and set off.

About 60km from Zumbo the river began to broaden into the lake proper, Cabora Bassa. Only a few km wide at first, the shoreline was hidden by thick beds of hyacinth weed with phragmites growing amongst it. These beds continued for miles and can sometimes be so completely congested as to make progress impossible.

We travelled close to the northern shore looking out for a rarely used camp set up by Pete Hougaard, said to be close to a hot spring, passing several fishermen in dugout canoes hollowed out from the Kigelia sausage tree', some up to 20ft long and quite deep and wide. Often they were miles from the shore tending to nets that were strung between logs that acted as markers and floats. Quite by chance we landed at a fisherman's hut that proved to be only a few hundred metres from the spring. The man was at first uneasy but soon relaxed and showed us his catch of bream and barbel that he was smoking and drying on a crude wooden rack. His bed was a simple reed mat, his only other possessions being a bag of salt and a transistor radio.

Larry and I headed inland to the lush green patch of grass that indicated the head of the spring. It was a dense vibrant green mass about knee-high, stretching for about 200m and extending to the base of a rocky hillside. Two or three rivulets of unpleasant sulphur smelling hot water gurgled in channels toward the lake. It was so hot that you couldn't put a hand in it. A number of young Illala palms grew in a cluster near the spring, completing this little green oasis in the midst of the dry grey brown of the surrounding shoreline.

I filmed Larry exploring the spring much as I'd done each time we came upon anything of interest or that deserved comment. This was done with the Sony Hi8 camera left for me by Chris Weber of National

Geographic. It was a frustrating camera to use, too light for my liking and far too automated with electronic facilities to simplify its use There were no T numbers or focus distances marked on the lens to enable pre-setting for a shot, which I found very limiting. However, it was light and small and surprisingly robust, suiting the needs of the trip very well.

Just over a ridge we found Pete's camp and the man who took care of it. He spoke good English and seemed genuinely pleased to see us – he'd been there for six months since his employer had last visited. His wife was an elegant, dignified looking woman who greeted us courteously in English. Such a surprise so far from anywhere.

Steve and Oskar were dozing in the shade of a small tree down near the boat as we arrived and we were just in time to see a canoe approaching at surprising speed. The five men aboard were grim faced and didn't look at all friendly. I was more than a little anxious to see that two of them wore military fatigues. When they landed and brought out an AK47 and a Tokorev pistol I felt sure that there was going to be trouble. Stories of shootings, kidnappings and muggings in war torn, lawless Mozambique, flooded through my mind.

The men must have been amused at how nonchalant we tried to be, as if it were quite normal to be confronted by armed men in the middle of nowhere on the northern shore of Cabora Bassa. One of the paddlers was a Zambian who spoke English and from him we learned that the armed men were Immigration officials from

Zumbo searching for illegal fish traders. They demanded our passports but Oskar brushed the request aside telling them that we were resident in the country and that our passports were back at our base at Chikoa. One man with yellow eyes and sharpened teeth didn't really like this explanation and wouldn't allow me to film them as they headed off into the bush.

By now the camp minder had prepared a meal for us from Steve's supplies so we sat down on the shore and ate Tastic rice and rump steak straight from two pots because thieves had stolen the plates and utensils from the boat the night before.

The immigration men returned carrying armfuls of dried fish extracted from some trader as a fine for not having the appropriate permits, and set off in their banana boat at surprising speed. The Zambian oarsmen being very efficient, strong paddlers.

The late afternoon skimming over the calm smooth lake was glorious. The mountains rose up in layers of blue and grey along the northern shore. The lake was vast and often we couldn't see the opposite shoreline. We stopped and swam in the deep water.

Shortly after a magnificent golden sunset we arrived at Magoa, a Kapenta fishing camp operated by two Zimbabweans on the southern shore about half way along the lake.

Our visit coincided with a charity tiger fishing contest. Fifty farmers from Karoi were in camp for the event.

A narrow steep sided sandstone gorge pock marked with caves led through to an enormous lagoon beyond.

On top of a 60ft cliff was the camp. About twenty speedboats lined the harbour and 4×4 bakkies were much in evidence. There were farmer fishermen everywhere, mostly in tatty shorts and little else, quaffing beer in alarming quantities. Late that evening we sat down to a meal of steak and baked potatoes but mine was gritty with sand and pretty much inedible so I escaped to get some sleep.

The first night of sleeping on the ground always takes some getting used to and the noisy antics of the farmers continued late into the night. Not a great night's sleep.

The next morning, around 5.30am the fishermen began preparing rods and boats for the day, and at 6am a bright flare announced the start of the contest and they were off into the lake at speed. The mayhem subsided, enabling us to pack and set sail ourselves.

The wind was up. We had been warned about this possibility but couldn't have anticipated the enormous waves that pounded toward us. White caps and troughs at least 5ft deep confronted our little boat as we headed East into the sun toward Steve and Oskar's base at Chikoa about 100km away.

An unusual weather system brought haze that hung like dense smoke over the horizon and we often couldn't see land. The boat leaped and plunged through these rough waters with surprising ease, but the jarring and banging made it almost impossible to sit down. After an eternity we reached the bay of Chikoa where about a dozen Kapenta fishing operations were based, about 30km from the dam wall and the town of Songa. It is a fairly desolate bay enclosed by a few small islands. The fishing camps were spaced a few km apart, their long drying racks never far from the shore. Freshly cut roads and odd buildings appeared out of the virgin bush where this new breed of pioneer were busy establishing a vibrant new enterprise. It was a hard, lonely life for the few white men who settled there. At the time there was no infrastructure of any sort so everything had to be imported from neighbouring countries. The potential rewards were, however, great for those with the determination and spirit to make it work. Steve at 20 and Oskar barely 25 seemed to me to have that will; I thought they were just mad enough to see it through.

The next afternoon Oskar took us into the gorge, right up to the site of the dam wall that holds back this massive body of water. The scale of everything there is awesome. The rock faces rise sheer and steep from the water, dark rock, ominous and strangely sinister, towering above. In many ways it is a scary place for the outsider.

The fear I sensed was hard to rationalise, perhaps partly because one felt so small between the massive walls. Or it may have had something to do with the recent long and bitter war that had been fought throughout the region and whose echoes still haunted the place. Larry said it looked as if God must have been angry when he created this gorge, the evidence of his displeasure was easy to imagine in the jagged cracks and dark rock walls towering over us where the wind buffeted around eerily.

Approaching the gorge there are steep mountains either side of the narrowing waterway. The rocky slopes are dotted with odd trees that cling on somehow. Amazingly, on these most unlikely, inhospitable and infertile slopes, there were people living, their tiny huts dotted high against the mountain sides. They had cleared the trees from between the rocks and planted their crops of millet and other grain in minuscule pockets of soil. Perhaps it indicates the desperation of a people ravaged by war and poverty or isolation and ignorance. Either way it defies logic. Even though the shoreline of this enormous dam resembles that of Kariba in Zimbabwe, there is no wildlife to be seen. Human habitation along the shore will probably mean that it will never return.

Our trip entailed the constant packing and unpacking of our effects and equipment, from truck to boat to truck and so on. It is the constant nightmare of film-makers, this packing of too much equipment into too small a place, over and over again. Larry remarked how the contents of our bags seemed to spread whenever we stopped, like some kind of living organism.

Another of our preoccupations was the constant attempt to avoid mosquitoes and malaria. We could ill afford to be stricken miles from help on the lower reaches of the river, in the mangroves or out at sea, so we carried nets, prophylaxis, repellents and treatments, but the stories of chloroquine resistant malaria are rife, and everyone knows someone who nearly died of it.

After a short stop in Chikoa we set off for Tete by road. A fish merchant flagged us down for a lift and we were grateful for his directions along some of the more obscure tracks through villages and on to join the main road. The wild countryside was beautiful and the fishermen's road was easy going. We passed young boys herding black and white cattle, and women picking Masau berries. In the villages there were small fat black pigs and goats and chickens. The soil looked rich and fertile. New fields were being carved out of the bush, trees had been chopped off at waist height and burned where they fell, all except the wild Masau trees which produced the reddish berries that were so sought after.

Charcoal was being sold along the roadside but few vehicles passed that way. We turned left at the tar road and climbed through hills, dodging potholes as we went. Some were so big that a car could disappear into them, and vegetation grew right up to crumbling verges. We turned left again onto the new highway that runs all the way from the Beira corridor north to Malawi. As we neared Tete, the countryside became more barren from the pressure of people. Eventually, only the baobabs remained and even they had been ravaged, with great strips of bark peeled off. On the outskirts of the town a smart, neat looking policeman in a crisp white shirt asked for Larry's driver's license before waving us on.

Tete was a sprawling mass of shanties surrounding the old Portuguese town. There was decay and dirt everywhere but the streets bustled with healthy looking people. We headed straight for Freitas Restaurant overlooking the Zambezi as it passes through the town. From the cool open veranda you can look on to the long suspension bridge that takes the road North. Freitas is a lively Hemingway sort of place where travellers, ex pats and local people gather to drink beer and eat piri piri chicken and swop stories. It is run by an American ex-Rhodesian soldier, Jesse Hickman, who seems to know everyone and everything in the area. His Mozambican wife, Maria, is related to a local chief and their establishment enjoys patronage of many prominent locals. We sat listening to Jesse's stories about the war days in this area and bizarre anecdotes about the terrible events during those times. He was also able to advise us on the state of the roads ahead.

We spent the night in a shared apartment in the town, the Junevendas. It was clean but shabby and in dire need of redecoration. Back at Freitas we drank beer with a group of ex pats and a local Mozambican UN representative. Next morning we made calls from the local post office where an efficient dialling system allowed us to report our progress back to Harare. The streets of Tete had a holocaust appearance, with the remnants of grand old buildings still standing, once elegant and stylish but now decayed. Money changers clutching bags of cash called out and followed us around offering good exchange rates for our Zimbabwe dollars, Rands and US dollars. They would appear from nowhere and crowd around whenever we stopped the vehicle.

Around midday on the 11th of August, four more kayakers arrived from Zimbabwe to join us. Our brightly coloured kayaks on the trailer and the enthusiasm of the whole group gave a festive air to our departure. Even the two traffic fines we received in the next 2km could not dampen our spirits, (one for not wearing seatbelts and the other for travelling over the bridge at 39 km/hr.)

We left the main highway 50km beyond Moatize after passing the wrecked remains of burned out Russian tanks lying in the bush. The dirt road took us South as we headed back towards the river beyond Doa. There was new settlement and bush clearing everywhere. The ruined remains of a railway line ran parallel to us much of the way – rusted rail tracks, some bent back on themselves and twisted into odd shapes. We were never able to figure out how this had been done on such a grand scale. Rail trucks lay on their sides or upside down as the bush engulfed them.

There were more people closer to the river, villages were springing up and huts were being constructed. An intricate skeleton of poles provided the framework often with an overhang to form a veranda for shade. At Sena a badly damaged bridge spanned several kilometres in arched sections over the wide river. A foreign engineering company was busy with reconstruction, replacing the parts destroyed during the war.

Travel after dark was not advised, incidents of armed banditry were common, so at last light we decided to set camp for the night.

Hoping not to alert the local people to our presence we turned off the road a few hundred metres into thick undergrowth, and quietly set about preparing food and putting up mosquito nets. We were not far from the village of Mutarara and from there on there were bound to be more people and more chance of discovery and trouble. It was an odd thing to be sitting silently in the dark eating what I hoped was bully beef while the voices of local villagers carried clear on the night air.

As the full moon rose we crept silently into our sleeping bags and tried to sleep. The crying shrieks of a night ape startled us a few times and the alarm snort of a bush-buck sounded like it was right among us. Later a strong wind picked up and blew the branches of the trees to cast moving shadows in the bright moonlight. It was not a relaxing night.

In the morning we crossed the Shire River on our way toward Morrumbala. The pontoon was a hand cranked affair operated by a cheerful crew. In front of us a magnificent mountain rose up from the flat ground. We bought boiled maize cobs in their husks for our breakfast and continued on around the base of the mountain. The remains of an extensive ranch from the colonial era straddled the road; dip tanks and concrete fence posts were still intact but the farm buildings were in ruins. At a junction in the road we bought fresh coconuts and sweet bananas from villagers. Food seemed plentiful but there were still several food aid distribution points along the way, sacks of maize from

Malawi covered in blue UN tarpaulins. Groves of green barked fever trees appeared between tall brachystegia.

At Morrumbala, a bustling market centre, we got directions from an Indian trader who spoke some English. We turned South again towards the road that would take us to Caia, the village on the Zambezi that was to be the start point of our epic kayak trip to the sea. From here progress was slow as the road deteriorated, damaged by trucks coming to recover the hard-woods that were being cut from the forest that we travelled through. Eventually we met the tar. It was an even more appalling road. Trenches had been dug every few kilometres, in some places every few metres. This was designed to keep Frelimo from using the roads north into Renamo areas during the war. Land mines had been placed in some of the holes as an added deterrent and we saw the twisted, rusting evidence of their effectiveness. This was the road to hell.

Before going too far along this miserable way, we reviewed our plans and decided instead to head north to Quelimane. By doing so we could remain together and make more satisfactory arrangements for our return trip. The next 160km were painfully slow as we wound our way around the tank traps, much slower than on the dirt road. Approaches to the many bridges were also dug up and the ramps onto them, treacherous for the unsuspecting driver. Our trailer developed a crack in a main strut. Still the countryside was grand, I kept expecting to see game but never did.

On the roadside villagers held up live chickens by their legs, waving them at us as we passed hoping to make a sale. Sometimes there were unidentifiable strips of dried meat for sale. Some of it was definitely cane rat.

It was a great relief to turn off this road at Nicuadala and onto the final stretch toward Quelimane. For the next 40km we passed an almost constant stream of people on the move. The flat open land either side of the raised causeway looked like soggy rice paddies with irrigation canals running off into the distance, small clumps of coconut palms and banana trees grew near the low thatched huts that dotted the landscape. It looked like a Hollywood version of Vietnam without the helicopters.

As we neared the town in the late afternoon the road became more congested and potholed until we were amongst the unkempt remains of the old Portuguese coastal town of Quelimane.

We waylaid a man driving a smart land cruiser who miraculously knew our only contact, the sainted Mr. Almeida, an official from Madal, a large copra producing company. This kindly Goanese gentleman went out of his way to help and allowed us to camp in the company's shipping offices for the night because there were no other rooms available. After a good meal of calamari and chicken at a noisy local restaurant we went back to the office and set about the important task of dividing and packing food and equipment into watertight dry bags in readiness for the kayak trip. It was a daunting task and before long every surface was

116

littered with our luggage. How it was to ever fit into the kayaks was a mystery to me. Finally, exhausted, we collapsed onto the office floor between the desks and enjoyed a good sleep. The next morning, water for our ablutions had to be fetched from the harbour in buckets and the unpleasant business of making the toilet flush became the unhappy task of Alistair who never let us forget it. Larry went off with Mr. Almeida to arrange a vehicle to carry us and the kayaks back to Caia while Mike Stewart went to have the damaged trailer welded

The rest of us sat drinking strong coffee overlooking the harbour on an overcast morning watching the dugouts come in on the tide. Small ships lay at anchor. Men selling chickens carried their pitiful wares in handfuls that hung upside down unprotesting as the vendors loitered about the pavements.

One constantly wondered what these towns must have looked like 30 years ago. The unkempt streets were like an unending set for an Indiana Jones movie where art directors had gone mad ageing every building and side walk. The surviving Portuguese colonial architecture tantalised the imagination, conjuring up the heyday of vibrant trade when the copra plantations thrived. In the town the shops were surprisingly well stocked with a wide variety of consumer goods, mostly from South Africa.

The plan was to leave our own transport in Quelimane for our return trip later, and so Larry had located a driver with a beaten up 5 ton truck to take us to Caia for US $140. The 160 km drive took until 8pm. Progress through the tank traps was painfully slow but without incident. That is, except for the weather front that brought ominous storm clouds across our path. We huddled up behind the cab when the rain began, the kayaks taking up most of the truck. When darkness fell we were all very conscious of the warnings about bandit ambushes, particularly since we had earlier passed an unfortunate victim of terrible brutality. The man had had his ears and lips and one hand cut off.

The last 20km was eerie in the dark. Fever trees glowed faint in the headlight (we only had one), and we passed the war-damaged ruin of a bridge whose remaining spans towered over us; the middle section lying in the gulley below. Fireflies blinked in the dark.

Part 2
The Kayak Adventure Begins

At Caia we unloaded our boats and gear next to the river at one edge of the settlement. A few people moved around in the shadows but paid us little attention. With some difficulty, using our small torches, we tried to arrange the kit into the kayaks for an early start, and set up nets against the swarms of mosquitoes. Local Mozambican music blared from a hut nearby and revellers could be heard across the river.

Attempted sleep was rudely broken by the sound of gunshots from the other side. We gathered around in the gloom trying to ascertain what was going on and what we should do. Much shouting and hysteria accompanied the shots. In minutes a group of men had gathered near our camp site as we all stood peering out at the river. It sounded as though boats were being paddled across to our side. The potential for trouble seemed great.

We decided against a hasty departure into the dark unknown. After a time a woman from Malawi told us that a thief had been caught and that the shots had come from the police. Still, we slept very lightly till 5am then hurriedly loaded and launched onto a misty river amongst large clumps of floating weed.

The sun rose on a magnificent expanse of river, golden sunrise streaming through the clouds. We were on our way at last. This was the first time I'd even sat in a kayak and I soon became painfully aware that it was not going to be as easy as I'd imagined. To start with I hadn't paid enough attention to distributing the bulk and weight properly, or arranged easy access to drinking water or cigarettes. My first hour was decidedly wobbly as water ran down the double ended paddle and made its way into my seat. Thankfully my colleagues were all very experienced kayakers and tutored me in the finer points during those first few hours. The sea-going Perception kayaks from New Zealand were surprisingly comfortable and user-friendly and I soon got the hang of it. The paddling was exhausting for a novice, and muscles I didn't know I had, ached.

Yet somehow we manage to reach our goal of 50km that first day.

We passed curious fishermen in dugout canoes, some who greeted us and many more who were suspicious. The current helped us along, we reckoned that it flowed at around 5 km/hr. Great clumps of hyacinth drifted along with us. Mountains faded into the distance and the surrounding land became flat and featureless. We passed a deserted mission, its church gutted from fire. Beyond that was Lacerdonia and Chupanga where Mary Livingstone had died of malaria and been buried beneath a great baobab tree.

By late afternoon the wind grew stronger and small waves washed over our kayaks as we searched for a suitable camp site for the night. We eventually found a hippo trail that led through an opening in the tall reeds. It was a good spot sheltered from the wind and obscured from view. Mosquitoes bit through our clothes, our jeans and long sleeve shirts providing little protection. The following morning Mike Stewart thankfully took my compliment of food in his kayak to make the going easier for me so that I could attempt to keep up. Alistair was already carrying my sleeping bag to give me more space for the video equipment which travelled between my knees. Filming from the kayak was slow and awkward; unpacking the camera from its dry bag and preparing it for use was time consuming and held up our progress considerably. The team were tolerant and drifted while I got the camera ready. Getting an acceptably steady shot from an unstable moving kayak was tricky, the only way to keep me from drifting around uncontrollably was to have Paul come alongside and hold me steady. For his sterling work in this capacity he became known as 'Tripod'. Another useful technique for travelling shots was to be towed from a short line but the paddle strokes still caused a certain amount of jerkiness. Needless to say, there was a good deal of paranoia about keeping the video camera dry - given their general aversion to any moisture that might cause the 8mm tape to jam in the delicate mechanism.

We breakfasted on our now customary bowl of Pronutro with heaps of sugar, powdered milk and raisins, as we dried out on a pretty sand bar. We filled our water containers and tripper bags, not knowing when we would encounter brackish tidal water from the sea. Purification tablets, one to a litre were dissolved into the containers as a precaution against the effluent that made its way into the river from all the towns and

121

villages. They seemed to be effective, as none of us suffered any stomach ills, even though a myriad of unidentified things lurked in our drinking water. The taste of chlorine was a small price to pay. The tripper bags resembled large medical 'drip' bags with long tubes attached and simple plastic clips to act as a tap. We each carried three of these bags, a supply of 12 litres. The tubes made it possible to drink on the move without having to take off your spray-deck and rummage for a water bottle, and they stowed conveniently in the narrow space forward of the rudder pedals.

A hard paddle followed to try and cover some distance and keep on schedule. A two-hour stretch before a rest and food stop was about all I could cope with while the others seemed happy to go on indefinitely, getting into a rhythm and paddling relentlessly. More than once I resorted to the emergency 'high energy' sachets that we carried, a sort of athlete's supplement that is rapidly absorbed into the bloodstream. They did keep me going but there were times when I teetered on the edge of total exhaustion.

We finally reached Marromeu, the deserted sugar mill and plantation that had once been the biggest in the world. We were told that the MNR had used it as a base and it now stood abandoned, its substantial rail siding stretching out along the shore.

That evening we set camp on a low sand bar with only a few reed clumps to shield us from view. The clear open sand of the island seemed a nice change from the previous night among the dense reeds. Sacred Ibis, flocks of red wing Pratincoles and graceful Skimmers were all around the sandy flats. It was the first time we'd seen so many water birds. The Pratincoles flew up in great flocks.

The night changed quickly from bright clear skies to a dense damp mist that drenched our equipment and soaked our sleeping bags. At midnight the moon glowed dim through the fog as we awoke to the sound of locals approaching. We stood silently listening to their paddles as the dugouts came closer. They were laughing and singing but all the same we suspected that they were trying to find us. Eventually, the voices receded and we went back to a damp sleep. Paul had wisely set up a tent and was the only one to stay dry.

Wet and uncomfortable we set off into the mist at first light to avoid discovery. It was a spectacular sight-seeing the sun rise through the fog. We paddled past Luabo on the southern bank, away from the town, to avoid potential bureaucratic problems, in the distance it appeared to be quite a substantial and busy place. An enterprising Mozambican paddled out to us in his dugout to trade. For the princely sum of two fish hooks and three cigarettes we acquired a dozen delicious bananas which made a welcome change from noodles and pilchards.

The countryside was changing character, we started seeing coconut palms and dense green lush vegetation, bananas and occasional maize patches.

We became preoccupied with locating what became known as the 'Chinde off-ramp', the most northern channel of the delta that would lead us to the town of Chinde and the ocean. We knew it couldn't be too far ahead. Huge flocks of Open billed Storks circled in thermals. Another 200 or so gathered on a sandbar with Sacred Ibis and a lone pelican. Getting close enough to film was an interesting business given that I couldn't hold the camera and paddle, so Mike had to tow me within range as Larry approached them. The shots were unacceptably wobbly but it was a lovely sight. By now my hands had started to cramp onto the paddle and the first ache of tendonitis crept up my wrists. Fortunately it was time for our midday stop. We washed ourselves in the river next to a long beach, put out our wet clothes and sleeping bags to dry and had our lunch. These stops were never leisurely, from the moment of landing to the time of launching back into the river there was a constant flurry of activity. To unpack the smallest thing entailed the opening of many watertight compartments and bags and everything was crammed into a specific little corner because of the limited space available. It still amazed me that we were carrying about 40kgs of equipment and provisions each. With the aid of a GPS Paul was able to determine that we were only about 2km from the Chinde channel as we started to speculate about mangroves and river sharks, tides and brackish water.

The channel turned out to be quite obvious and much larger than expected, not unlike the full scale river we'd been on. A pair of Palm nut Vultures reeled overhead and the first tidal mud flat came up on our left. More flocks of waterfowl congregated on the open mud, mainly Openbills and Ibis but also Egyptian Geese, Spurwing and other smaller waders. The channel was wide and meandering with occasional coconut palms but the shoreline became a dense mass of tall reeds and mud. The sunset that evening was spectacular through scattered cloud but we still hadn't found a suitable place to camp. We scoured the shoreline with increasing desperation as darkness descended – finding only mud in this tidal area.

At last a place was chosen amongst a thick grove of banana trees. The bank was 5ft high. Hauling the laden kayaks off the water and up the sheer bank required gargantuan effort. Even before we were ashore we were inundated with swarms of mosquitoes, being in shorts and T-shirts we were bitten mercilessly. There was frantic scrambling for repellent that we smeared all over ourselves. In the gloom we hacked out a small area and slid the boats between the trees to give ourselves room. We had to cover ourselves as best we could against the relentless mosquitoes. It was a strange looking pitiful group indeed that squatted around the gas burner for supper with balaclavas or jacket hoods over our heads. After the mixed pilchards, bully beef, noodles and tinned veg we crept exhausted into our beds amidst the dense undergrowth. Our bedtime story telling included a new respect and sympathy for the GIs in Vietnam who must have served for months at a time in conditions like this. There was also a good deal of black humour about bird eating spiders, snakes and other jungle dwelling nasties. Bats hunted in the dark, swooping amongst the banana trees, a dugout passed just below the bank and drums echoed across the river. Just when I thought it couldn't get worse it began to rain. Larry and I slept outside but the others had put up tents against the mosquitoes. The plastic 'space blanket' that I threw over myself covered me to the knees. I lay in the dark as the water soaked through my sleeping bag slowly but inexorably creeping up toward my waist. By morning I lay in a shallow muddy puddle.

The channel was about 45 km long and we were already well along it that disastrous night. In the morning, moving on a fast outgoing tide, for which I was eternally grateful, we made good speed. We could hear the roaring of the ocean long before we saw it. A rain filled slate grey sky on our right provided a dramatic backdrop to a seemingly endless flock of storks that flew in a thin open line, palms framed in the foreground.

We stopped alongside a large dugout filled with people to ask how far it was to Chinde. A man wearing a Russian military hat stared at us with glowering disapproval but said nothing. We rounded a wide bend and there in the distance was the Indian Ocean, the sky met the sea on a seamless horizon. In front of us the twin masts of a wreck protruded from the water. A fisherman using a hand line watched us pass with amused fascination. The shoreline vegetation had changed completely to a dense mangrove swamp. The final approach to Chinde was littered with rusting wrecks, some quite substantial, that lay strewn up the beach in a tangle of rusted barnacled metal.

People appeared from nowhere and watched as we paddled past; small raggedy children ran along the beach to watch us land. By the time we reached the handful of roofless and derelict yellowed buildings a few adults had come down onto the beach to greet us. It was a wonderful moment. Everyone was in good spirits and very curious to see us and even more curious to see the Kayaks and our equipment. It was a happy good-natured affair with much hand shaking and laughter. I felt a great sense of achievement. We had paddled 150 km through the Zambezi delta and arrived safely. It was 11.30am on Wednesday the 16th of August.

Larry went off in search of the Harbour master while I sat on my kayak surrounded by children looking out to sea, knowing that I would always remember this moment.

Mr Ali was the harbour master, a most hospitable man, large and moustachioed and good-natured. He immediately invited us to his home for a meal and wouldn't hear of us continuing on our journey till the next day. He pointed to the rain-filled sky and shook his head saying 'tempest, tempest'. Before long he had organised for us to stow the kayaks in a dilapidated shed and arranged for a man to keep watch over them. He lived in one of the many Portuguese-built houses that survive throughout the small town of Chinde. We sat around in a circle as he introduced his wife and baby, a gurgling 9-

month-old named Sakina. Conversation was awkward because of the language problem, further complicated by the intercession of a very willing young man called Morgan who tried to act as interpreter. Sadly, his self-taught English was about as effective as our Portuguese, and only led to more confusion. Brunch was duly served at the large dining room table by a disabled elderly servant who shuffled about taking instructions from Mrs Ali. The meal of rice, beef and fried eggs was better than anything we'd eaten on the trip, but the starter was a little disconcerting. It was a grey pasty, lumpy soup of indefinable content, the texture alone almost made me gag, but the others seemed to wolf it down, and so in the interests of politeness I persevered. Days later I learned that everyone else had also fought back a similar reaction to retch. That afternoon Mr. Ali took us on a grand tour of Chinde town. It was a delightful place with the ambiance of a seaside resort, palm trees dotted about the neatly laid out town. Old buildings with wide cool verandas lined the few streets. There is a village square and a grand admin building with a wide stairway up to a balcony that looks out over the street. Like every other town we saw, it was run down and in need of massive restoration and redecoration but somehow it retained an old world charm. The market was grubby and chaotic. Tiny fish lay in rows next to shrimp curling in the sun and smelling terrible with swarms of flies buzzing noisily. There wasn't much on sale, a few pathetic little displays of goods in front of each vendor, soap, bad milk powder, expensive candles, cassava and maize meal from Malawi. I spent most of my time trying to extricate myself from the attentions of the village idiot who shouted a lot and sprayed me with spittle. Larry negotiated for rice and sugar to replenish our supplies.

Mr. Ali took us to the police and to some other local authorities to comply with the local protocol before arriving at the town bar. We drank Vivo beer from tins as the friendly locals came to check us out. It was the first time we'd relaxed in days. We were exhausted. Our tour continued past the collapsing prison that resembled an old fortress to the almost well-kept cemetery. The headstones were a fascinating glimpse into the past. Among the graves of Portuguese administrators and dignitaries were those of sailors who perished off the coast, and missionaries from before the turn of the century. Young British naval officers and a vice consul lay buried with elaborate epitaphs inscribed in stone. The faded sepia photographs of the dead adorned some of the gravestones. A lighthouse, or at least a beacon, stood amongst the palms nearby. Shanties of palm thatched huts lined paths a short way from the old streets, people bustled about their business and greeted us as we passed.

Mr. Ali had made arrangements for us to dine with him again that evening. An unfortunate duck had been slaughtered in our presence for the occasion, something that I could have done without. He had also arranged for us to spend the night in the town 'guest house', complete with real beds, a shower and sit down toilet.

Absolute luxury. The house was a huge rambling place with four bedrooms and even mosquito screens on the windows. The old furniture and light fittings reflected its former grace. On our way back past the bright yellow little 'Maritime Office' in the dark, Morgan our erstwhile translator tried to engage me in some deep and meaningful conversation which I couldn't make head nor tail of. I understood odd words which he kept repeating. Ninja's in black clothes, white men sucking blood, Quelimane. When I indicated that I had no idea what he was on about, he became very agitated. He began to stutter and clutched at my arm pointing at the veins and repeating 'blood, blood'. The others had long since given up on him and I was too tired for this guessing game. I ignored him and wrote it off to some movie he must have seen.

Dinner was interesting, the duck was tough and almost inedible, but Mr Ali and his wife were incredibly hospitable. We drank beer while Bryan Adams and Bon Jovi played on a cassette deck. Mrs Ali was getting louder and quite festive, and she produced a gallon container of sweet local palm brew which we were all obliged to drink, complete with ants that floated on the surface of the milky white fluid. Larry's bed collapsed during the night but none of us heard a thing.

Thursday 17th August 1995. I think half the town came to see us off that morning. We'd had to repack, making sure that everything was watertight for the open sea, and spent a good deal of time tying everything down so it wouldn't float away if we capsized. After much hand shaking and bear hugs from Mr. Ali we waved our farewell to the good people of Chinde and set off across the wide river mouth to the sand bar that marked the entrance to the ocean. It took an hour to cross and gave us all time to ponder what the sea might have in store for us on the 100 km Journey North to Quelimane.

Part 3
Hairy Days and Hairy Nights

We beached on the sand bar and looked out onto the open ocean and the pounding waves for the first time. For Larry it was the culmination of his epic 2700 km journey from the Zambezi source to the sea. It was an exciting moment filled with emotion as he took a small phial of water he'd carried from the source and ceremoniously poured it into the ocean at the mouth of the river. The journey had taken him three months. The dream he'd nurtured into reality had been fulfilled. I filmed the event for posterity and watched him run out into the surf and dive through a breaking wave.

After drying off, he sat with his sketchpad and painted a simple watercolour of the scene before us. The spit of open sand with the river on the right and the open sea to the East. Larry summed up the moment, saying that it wasn't so much what he'd done that excited him, but what he'd seen along the way.

The tide had just turned as we faced the kayaks into the waves and paddled furiously to break through the surf. Mike and Craig were experienced sea kayakers and instructed the rest of us on what to expect. I went over the first small waves quite easily but each succeeding one seemed to double in size. With head down I crashed through the next one as it broke over the kayak, pushing me off the line to meet the next monster at a right angles.

Salt water stung my eyes and I could just hear someone yelling 'paddle, paddle, harder, harder!'

Without a moment to spare the nose came round to meet the next wave. It looked very big. Next instant it was on top of me, on top of me and all around me. In a swirling boiling frenzy I felt the kayak lift and falter. Suddenly I was through. Blinking and shaking my head like a dog to get the water out of my face I saw that the next wave had a smooth rounded shoulder. We were all safely through the line of breakers. We were now in a deep swell that lifted us up and dropped us down into the troughs about 8ft deep. It was exhilarating. We headed north to about 100m outside the breakers and 400m from the shore. The going was surprisingly easy. We estimated we must have been going at about 7kph.

After a two-hour paddle the aches and hunger pangs were back and we decided to head for shore to brew up some tea and have our midday meal. Unthinking, I turned toward the shore and waited for the biggest wave I could find. I mean, how difficult could this be?

The big one rose up and surged toward me. I paddled madly. Suddenly its power was beneath me. I was at the crest of a giant wave that was breaking. I was on top of the world racing along at great speed. The thrill was indescribable. Only surfers know this sensation.

Then I was hurtling down the glassy curve of water, still elated, but now the nose of the kayak started to dig in. The surf roared just behind me, the back of the kayak lifted, the nose dug in further till it reached my spray deck. Wipe out.

133

I can now imagine what it would be like for an ant to be inside a washing machine. I had no control whatsoever as the surf pummelled me for an eternity, spinning the kayak over and over, spilling the contents over and over again. I found the surface just in time for the next wave to punish me once more. My next recollection is that of my concerned colleagues being at my side. Satisfied that I'd not drowned, they turned my kayak upright and helped me to shore as I watched the camera bag bobbing in the surf.

I was not the only one to have suffered such indignity. Paul had watched me go from behind the breakers, waiting in case I needed help. Seeing me leave in apparent control, he turned back to wait for a suitable moment to ride in. He was caught mid-turn and found himself looking up at the sky as a huge wave shifted the nose of his kayak. Too late to power through it, the wave lifted him up and over in a backward somersault before driving him down to the sea bed with a crunch that buckled the kayak and sent him sprawling into the surf. Miraculously no one had been injured and nothing was lost.

The white, palm fringed beach stretched as far as the eye could see, it was beautiful. We dragged the kayaks up the sand and put out things to dry while we prepared food. Out of nowhere local people began to appear. They were good natured and curious as they gathered round to see the kayaks and equipment. Unlike Anglo Saxons these people had no sense of privacy or personal space, and they soon crowded in, often standing amongst the utensils, and uncomfortably close. They laughed and pointed in amazement and would not go until we packed and headed back to sea.

Back out in the swell, my worst fear came to plague me, seasickness. The nausea built up, making me dizzy and weak, each paddle stroke became an immense effort till I could no longer stop myself from retching. Larry had held back to keep me company and steadied my boat while I threw up. Trying to lean over the side only threatened to capsize the boat so I had no choice but to vomit all over my spray deck. It was my lowest moment. Fortunately the water washed over the deck. I dreaded continuing in the relentless motion of the swell but somehow recovered quite rapidly and was able to go on.

I was a little less reckless on the next landing and almost made it to shore, riding along the wave and bracing against it with the paddle. But while congratulating myself on my skill, a small wave caught me off balance and roiled me in the surf once more.

That night we camped above the beach amongst low dunes not far from where the Bazar River flows into the sea. To save our dwindling gas supply we had taken to building fires to cook on and had a fine blaze going by the time the sun- set. As usual, curious people materialised out of nowhere. After the usual exchange of greetings, close scrutiny of everything in camp followed before four men sat down at the fireside. They seemed very content to just sit there and watch us eat. It was very strange. Sometime after they left, three new strangers approached through the darkness. We probably wouldn't have heard them but for the scrape of a panga being drawn from its sheath. I turned the beam of the small torch toward the sound and saw the glint of a blade. The three men froze. I think someone shouted. One of the men who was away to one side ran. A moment later his two fellow lurkers also took to their heels and vanished beyond the dunes into the dark.

Somewhat disconcerted by this turn of events we decided that it would be a sensible precaution to take turns at guard duty to keep watch while the others slept. We reviewed our very limited defensive arsenal, two pencil flare guns, three cans of Mace, a whistle and the knives that each of us carried. We then drew matches to determine who would take what shift. That settled we carefully inspected our surroundings and discovered that Alistair's mattress had been stolen. I think it was the only thing that was stolen on the whole trip.

Then we heard people approaching. It was our four fireside friends. One of them, Zusi, spoke a little Fanigalo or Chilapalapa. We told him about the visitation and our concerns and he and his friends agreed to spend the night at our fire, I remember listening to the four of them chatting away as I fell asleep.

My exit out through the surf the next morning was a disaster. At a critical moment the last and biggest breaking wave before the open sea dumped its full weight and fury right on top of me. Somehow I was still upright, but things were mightily wrong. My kayak was

136

wallowing beneath the surface. My spray deck had popped, opening the kayak which had filled in an instant. I floundered around at the mercy of the waves with no control at all. Suddenly Mike Stewart was beside me, he yelled at me to swim for shore and took control of my sorry craft, somehow manoeuvring it back to the shallows. The others waited patiently beyond the breakers. This was the hard way to learn about the function of a small flat aluminium bar that I was supposed to have slipped through the spray deck.

We knew from our maps that a spur of sand protruded out into the ocean at the mouth of the Rio Linde, the chart indicated breakers. The swell was bigger than we'd experienced so far and in the distance we could see the white tops of the breakers stretching far out to sea. By the time we were close enough to inspect this new peril the waves were enormous, around three metres high. Tired as I was from the long hard paddle and my unplanned swim earlier that morning, we realised that there was no choice but to go around. The breakers were bigger than anything we'd anticipated. If any one of us had come out of their boat in those conditions, a deep-water rescue would have been impossible. As it was we stuck close together and agreed that a flare should be fired on the hour if we became separated.

Moving as close as we dared to the edge of the breakers we headed out to sea. Although not actually breaking, the waves we were going over towered above us. I watched the front halves of the kayaks rise off the

137

water and hang airborne for a moment as my fellows crested the waves, before careening down into deep troughs. For a while it was an enormous thrill, but to stay upright and meet each wave correctly required concentration and hard work. Now odd waves were also coming from the side and we called out warnings to each other so as not to be caught unawares.

The end of the breakers didn't seem to get any closer. My legs ached, a point on each heel felt raw, stomach and back muscles burned, the tendons in my wrists sent searing pains up into my forearms. Even though I wore gloves, blisters swelled where my fingers protruded from the cut off ends. Cramp closed my grip on the paddle. I knew I was dehydrating, unable to drink because of the seasickness that ejected everything from my stomach. There was nothing I could do but keep going or drown.

An eternity later we skirted the fringe of the breakers and once again paddled parallel to the distant coast. We were about 15 km from land. Someone saw a shark, someone else confirmed it. Suddenly I was underneath my kayak, dark water all around me. I must have been caught off balance. I spluttered to the surface. The kayak was upside down, but somehow, I reached over and pulled it upright. Clawing at the cockpit lip I hauled myself back in. Mike Stewart was the first to reach me but the others were close behind. He shouted for a container to bale with. The monster waves kept coming. We baled frantically, aware that the next wave could capsize us both. Somehow we got enough of the water out for me to continue. The whole episode had only

138

taken a few minutes and I'd only been in the water for seconds. I remember looking around at my five companions a short while later very grateful in the knowledge that each man was totally dependable and that every one of them had had a hand in saving me from disaster. It was a good feeling.

Larry fed me two sachets of the hi-energy paste. It was late and we still had a very long way to go. The sun was setting when we finally made the shore and dragged the kayaks up the beach. We had paddled without rest for four hours. Exhausted but elated with a sense of achievement, we set camp and prepared food in the dark.

As before, a small crowd of locals came from nearby huts to inspect us. We'd asked for fresh water and they returned instead with a container of palm brew. They had obviously been imbibing themselves, and soon left when we declined the offer. Alistair had noticed that the people here looked different, perhaps from another tribe.

A crude meal over, Alistair, Paul and Craig went down to the water's edge to wash the dishes. I fussed around the fire preparing tea and paid little attention to the hubbub of voices coming from where Larry was unpacking and preparing his bedding. The voices suddenly grew louder and more agitated, I could see a large group of people confronting Larry and more gathering in the shadows. As I went over to see what the commotion was about Larry said that we had trouble and to get the others back so that we could stick together. There was something sinister in the mood of this crowd that we hadn't encountered before. I ran down to the others explaining only that there was a ruckus back up at our camp.

We got back to find that the crowd had continued to grow, they now completely surrounded Larry and stood in noisy groups amongst our kit that had been laid out for sleep. Larry was trying in vain to reason with a big square headed man who shouted at the top of his voice gesticulating wildly. There was a terrible air of hostility and aggression that ran through the crowd. I grabbed a paddle and pushed my way through to Larry noticing for the first time that most of the men carried pangas. We grouped together trying to make sure that no one could surprise us from behind. By now it seemed that everyone was shouting, more people streamed down the bank to join the men. The sweet smell of palm brew was everywhere. Still more kept coming, some carried spears. Women and teenagers now joined in haranguing us from all sides.

I searched the faces that pressed in on us, trying to find reason where none existed. Paul who was the most accomplished linguist among us tried to communicate in Portuguese. I searched around asking if anyone could speak Chilapalapa. By now the troublemakers around Larry were rifling through the bags, throwing them onto the ground and demanding that Larry open them. My own stuff was strewn about in the sand. A woman started to scream hysterically which only inflamed the men even more. A couple of the men had torches which they shined in our faces and at the growing mound of our possessions that was being inspected. There seemed to be a deliberate movement to split us up as each of us was completely surrounded. I clutched the knife in my jacket pocket with very gloomy thoughts about confronting at least one of the ringleaders.

Suddenly there was more screaming as the torchlight fell on our first aid supplies, the syringes evidently being the cause of widespread hysteria. Men were still pulling my bags from the watertight compartment of the kayak. Faces leered out of the darkness and the shouting continued all around.

The mob had grown to about 200 including women and children. Up till now we had all tried to keep calm, careful not to inflame the situation and provoke violence. But the ringleaders, about six of them, would not let up. Larry was being provoked beyond reason; he suddenly changed tactics and shouted back at them, pushing them away. For a moment they fell back surprised as we quickly began gathering our kit. He shone his torch at the panga in a man's hand yelling at him demanding to know what the hell he intended to do with it. The man reacted sheepishly, almost embarrassed.

Paul, Alistair and the others had quietly been packing up whilst this madness raged around us. Now realising the utter futility of our predicament Larry and I hastily threw the remaining equipment into the kayaks. Nothing was packed into their protective dry bags. The mob surged around louder and more aggressive than ever. We had no choice but to make a dash for the sea.

141

As we dragged our kayaks across the sand the mob followed chanting and howling but apparently pleased that we were leaving.

I knew that there was no way of making it through the breakers in the dark; my kayak was stuffed with kit so that I could not get into it. The angry mob physically drove us into the water. As I waded into the surf with the others I stripped off my heavy clothes fully expecting to have to abandon my boat and swim for it.

The frenzied mob did not follow us into the sea. By the time it was waist deep my kayak had turned over and was completely filled with water making it heavy and unwieldy to drag through the small breakers. For a time I couldn't see the others, only the dark shapes of our tormentors against the sand. Struggling to make headway along the beach as the surf pulled at my capsized boat, I could see no way out of this bizarre predicament. I caught up to the others and we continued along the beach chest deep. The crowd followed on the shore. I suppose we must have gone on like that for over an hour covering little more than a kilometre.

The only consolation was that the crowd was now somewhat reduced. We were all painfully aware that our lot was not improving. Larry decided that there was no option but to try and reason with the men who followed us and waded out of our sight toward them. We grouped together holding the boats. Standing there in the water I counted the heads of 60 men. I also became aware of how cold I was. Naked and wet, my teeth started to chatter in the cool breeze. Great! Hypothermia to add to exhaustion and exposure. I also became painfully aware that the video equipment was now floating in some corner of my kayak and that the shot tapes were probably ruined. The record of Larry's journey was being destroyed by seawater as we stood there – two weeks work down the drain.

By now we were getting anxious about Larry, he'd been gone for some time. For all we knew he might have been hacked to death. Paul went to investigate. It was frustrating beyond reason to stand there helpless, not able to hear anything above the noise of the surf, not knowing what was happening less than a hundred metres away.

Larry in the meantime had managed to communicate with someone who had worked on the mines in South Africa. Speaking Fanigalo, he was able to state our case and eventually the man offered to go into a nearby village and locate a local council or party official. The hysteria had died down as we regrouped and waded into shallower water where we could at least sit on our kayaks. A long game of patience followed, our bedraggled group soaked and tired watched by the shadowy figures on the shore.

Eventually, the 'secretary' arrived and began to disperse the remaining men. Reluctantly, the crowd began to break up and disappear into the night, leaving only six men who were part of the Secretary's retinue. They agreed to stay with us as a precaution against any renewed trouble and went off to gather firewood while we emptied the water from the kayaks and set camp on the beach.

My sleeping bag was the only dry thing that I had. We lay between the kayaks and went to sleep. The last thing I remember was hearing an agitated scratching noise under my soggy mattress. A crab was trying to emerge from its hole in the sand. Too bad.

A couple of hours later in the first glow of dawn we broke through the surf into the open sea as people started to appear on the beach and walk towards us. We paddled into the sunrise very happy to be alive. Ahead of us, the large open inlet leading to Quelimane was marked by a buoy. We rounded it on a smooth glassy sea as the tide turned and we landed on a beautiful wide sandy beach. I barely had the strength to drag my kayak up the sand.

We ate and drank tea and put our kit out to dry as we tried to assess the damage to equipment and our losses from the last twelve hours. A spray deck and a pair of jeans had been lost in the sea. The video camera batteries had shorted and the terminals had been corroded away in the process, only two had survived and one of those was flat. Two out of five videotapes were soaked. A stills camera and Walkman recorder were beyond repair. We were unbelievably tired but unscathed. I filmed brief interviews with each of our team, not knowing if the camera was still able to record.

I dreaded the final 25 km paddle into Quelimane as the rigours of the previous day and night took their toll on aching muscles. The tide worked in our favour but I seriously doubted my ability to paddle for another three hours in the gathering heat. There was not a breath of wind as the channel narrowed between the mangroves. In the distance, a tug guided a large ship into the channel and we turned course to intercept it, hoping beyond hope that we might catch a ride with it to the harbour, still some 20 km away. Mike separated from us racing across into the path of the tug. With the promise of a bottle of whiskey for the captain, the tugboat Casa Maq allowed us on board. Where the strength to haul the kayaks up onto the crowded deck came from I do not know, but we managed to lash them on top of each other and find space for ourselves. I can't remember being that relieved before. I would have bought the captain a dozen cases of whiskey if he'd asked for it.

Just off the Madal harbour we lowered the boats back into the water and bade the crew a very grateful farewell. We landed on the concrete slipway and carried the kayaks back up to Mr. Almeida's office where Larry's Landcruiser was parked. Our Kayak journey was over.

The explanation for the hostile reception that we received that miserable and terrifying night is almost as unbelievable as the event itself. Part of the answer may lie in what Morgan tried to warn us of that night in Chinde. Apparently there is a belief amongst the people of that particular area that white people come under cover of darkness to suck the blood of the natives. This was confirmed by a Mozambican of Portuguese descent who lived in Quelimane. Evidently, the people had been terrified of us. White men emerging from the sea at nightfall in strange craft carrying unfamiliar medical equipment may well have been too much of a coincidence and confirmation of their belief. Further to this, many of the younger people had probably never seen a white man. Then add a liberal amount of palm wine to stir the imagination and distort reason and you have the formula for a nightmare.

As to the origin of this 'taboo' we can't be sure except that it sounds suspiciously like something a political commissar might say: *'the white men are returning to Mozambique and they will suck you dry'*.

The next day we started on the long drive home. It took all day to reach the port of Beira, crossing the Zambezi by pontoon at Caia where our kayak journey had begun. Two punctures, a broken trailer and a few roadblocks later we arrived at a very pleasant beach camp-site with good food, beer and hot running water. Absolute luxury. From Beira it was only eight hours to Harare.

Post Script: The videotapes dried out and the images were fine. Much of the footage was used by National Geographic in a programme called 'Explorers Journal", an account of Larry's journey from the source of the Zambezi to the sea.

Wildlife Miniature
Susie Cottrell

In the farmhouse beside the Mupfure River whose waistline changes dramatically through the seasons I had a wide and comfy bed, netted against mosquitoes, into which our series of pet pookies made their way during the early hours, especially on cold winter mornings after a night of hunting. They would snuggle under the duvet close to my body with cold hands and feet and lie absorbing my warmth.

These delightful little bush babies, *aka* night apes, lived entirely independent of us and only sought our company when it suited them, sometimes on cold nights draped on one of us while we watched TV, having a sip of beer at sundowner time or in the morning, gratefully eating baby porridge prepared especially for them.

Oh, the thrill of waking to the river all swollen and thundering over the weir in January, spreading up the sandbank, bending the reeds; even at times carrying whole trees in the surge. It was on such a night that I was woken by Pookie running up and down beside me in the bed. He was unusually restless. As I could hear lots of calls near the open window, I assumed he was afraid of a wild pookie. This went on for several minutes so I turned on the light. Nothing to be seen.

Pookie goes quiet and climbs out and sits on my pillow looking round with his enormous eyes. To my utter astonishment I can feel 'something' in bed next to me. I lifted the sheets cautiously and stared in wonder at a

147

tiny Gollum-like creature crouched in the dark. Our pookie boy was a pookie girl and I was chosen to baby-sit whilst mum went out hunting. The surge of emotion I felt!

Mum disappeared and I lay in a state of euphoria, babysitting, waiting for dawn. She reappeared an hour later and, snatching the baby, sprang onto the cupboard where she hid with it under a cap. Excitement in the house was intense. We knew not to disturb her and waited with anticipation for evening time and the new mum to make a move. Sure enough she came to me in the sleeping dark and once more left her precious bundle while she went out foraging.

I called the family at dawn and we photographed and tried to touch the spitting, hissing baby until mum disturbed us and, in a fit of pique, once more snatched the baby and fled into a large clay pot resting on top of the wardrobe.

I was no longer 'the trusted one' and from then on she kept the baby hidden from us during her nightly excursions.

Some weeks after baby was mobile – we watched her growing with constant interest – she escaped from the bedroom window one dark night without her doting mother's permission. Mother came to me soon afterwards quite obviously frantic and keening in distress. As clearly as one can speak animal to human she told me that baby had gone out of the window into the wild outdoors where all manner of terrors lurked. Like Eagle owls, who we regularly heard calling and on one occasion saw no less than 5 perched together in a clump of Mufuti trees swaying above the lawn. There were also the giant bush babies who screamed from the treetops every night. And who knows what other terrors!

I was speaking English to her and trying to calm her. I gestured to her to go out and look for her baby, holding the fly screen open and indicating to her to go out. She got my meaning, and sometime later came back, proudly clutching the baby to show me.

Those utterly wonderful animals spent several years living and roaming freely with us in our environment, and we were so much richer for knowing them.

Snakes Alive
Susie Cottrell

Last week while I was away an unknown predator killed a hen sitting on eggs on the veranda of the house on the farm near Chegutu. The family woke to blood and feathers. Our cook, Musa, was straight way instructed to break one egg and show the contents to two-year-old Sophia and bury the rest. 'Aah', she says, 'A dead chicken'.

Then on Wednesday at dusk Gray and I heard a terrible squawking. We rushed out to see what was happening. There, in a flower bed in the garden, we found a hen staggering around and gurgling her last. He lifts her from the *agapanthus* and she collapses in his hands, dead. A snake no doubt.

We call for a golf club and torch, and poke around and quickly find a clutch of eggs under an abandoned kitchen unit. Further moving and poking reveals a greyish snake. We shout for the guard who runs over with his catapult. The snake tries desperately to hide in the shadows but we force it out with the 9-iron and the guard kills it with one shot. A Mozambican Spitting Cobra.

The children in pyjamas cluster round, hysterical with terror and excitement as snake blood drips onto the pathway. Oliver holds it by the tail. It is about a metre long. Sophia climbs as high up me as she can.

Aaah!

Next evening at dusk the puppy Pricklth (so named by lisping Sophia) is foraging in the flower bed. She yelps, and a giant eagle owl rises on silent wings and floats across the lawn. Pricklth tears to the safety of the veranda.

Phew!!

Next morning Sophia declares that during the night the owl tried to bite her finger off and she needs a plaster. Bad dream for a two-year old.

That day Nicholas reports much commotion and bleating from the Mupfuri riverbank below the paddock. On investigation he finds a croc has seized a goat and disappeared with it; and this is the river where everyone has been so confidently assuring us that it is fine to swim in because crocs don't like the noise we make. Hmmmm!

I return to Harare on Monday.

Thursday Sophia phoned at 6am in a state, to tell me that there was another snake, and an owl, and the dog involved in some story. The truth emerges. At dusk once again the eagle owl tries to snatch Pricklth from the flower bed and once again she tears to the safety of the veranda. But in the dead of night Jade and Graham are woken from deep sleep to terrible cries from the veranda. They sense at once it is a snake attack. There is a power cut so they scrabble with torches to find clothes and keys. Gray emerges onto the veranda to dead silence. Jade refuses to see her puppy dying from a snake bite so she hovers by the doorway.

In the torchlight a huge python lies coiled on the dogs' bed with Pricklth's hind feet just visible at the edge of its jaws.

Gray flies up the steps and with both hands grasps the snake's coils. Immediately it regurgitates the wet and motionless puppy.

Much yelling and confusion ensues. Jade finds a golf club and Gray smacks the snake which grasps the head of the club and coils its body up the shaft.

Gray lifts the club, complete with angry snake, and shouts to Jade: 'Resuscitate the puppy!'

'No!' she screams. 'You resuscitate the puppy'.

She is not the resuscitating type.

Gray drops the snake over the edge of the veranda onto the grass and turns his attention to the lifeless puppy. He feels a tiny heartbeat and begins what he hopes is CPR – pressing on the heart area with regular prods.

Oliver assured me in his account of the events, that 'Pricklth was dead but my dad brought her back to life'.

Jade is running back and forth past the angry hissing snake with towels and other emergency stuff to revive the dog. After a few minutes the puppy arches back, gasps once then lies still. Gray thinks it is all over. But the python begins sliding back up the steps to reclaim its meal and Gray shouts to Jade to bring another golf club from the pitch black basement, which I assure you is a scary enough place in broad daylight.

All the while Gray is yelling that he is under attack.

He fends off the reptile and at this moment Pricklth opens her eyes and moves. She is terrified and shocked, but staggers about. Jade whisks her into the safety of the lounge whilst Graham whacks the snake. They try to take photos of it but in the dark the camera lens is unable to focus.

After about an hour of soothing and petting, the puppy is calm enough to sleep. They check on the snake. It has vanished.

Snuggled into Gray in their bed, Pricklth sleeps, but she wakes frequently jumping and whimpering. She stinks of chemicals, probably the mix of python digestive enzymes and stomach acid.

In the morning the pup seems fine; sound in limb and eating, though she has one bloodshot eye and remains shocked and terrorised.

Sargy, the Scotty (Scotty cross JR) puppy, who legged it at the first sign of trouble in the night, has been found safe outside the back door. He is clearly not the great home defender. Anyway it seems that the chicken killer was probably the python which has now disappeared off the front lawn and will no doubt be back to capture something else in the future.

I arrive on the farm on Friday and struggle to believe that the little puppy now wriggling and yapping at my feet, and perfect in every way, spent so much time unconscious in the inner regions of a hungry snake.

Nothing dull around here.

The Farmer and the Farmer's Wife
Author unknown

On May 6, 2008 soon after mid-day I was visited by three men at our farm between Chegutu and Kadoma. They told me that I had two minutes to vacate the property or they would send in the mob. They said the house was not worth sacrificing our lives for, because we *would* lose our lives. They said they were like hungry lions.

My wife went and made a report to the Chegutu Police Station about the incident, naming the people involved. I asked them if they would react to any incident and they informed us that they would speak to the Assistant Inspector.

At about 1 pm that day a white Datsun 1800 pick-up arrived at the gate with about 12 people. They demanded that I open the gate because they wanted to talk to me. I refused and went into the house with my wife and we locked ourselves in. They then came to the house and wanted me to go outside to speak to them which I also refused to do.

They started smashing windows and then the front door.

One of them pointed a single barrel shotgun inside the house at us upstairs where we were. He fired a shot, obviously intended to kill us. After the shot he went out and it went quiet for a while and then we heard three shots coming from the workers' housing area. The mob returned with all the workers and fired another shot outside.

I managed to get through to the Assistant Inspector at the Chegutu Police Station to ask for assistance. He told me to phone him back in half an hour. Throughout all of this my wife was phoning friends in the hope they could get help for us from the police. All without result. We also tried several times to get through to the Member-in-Charge on his cell phone, but he did not answer.

By this time it was dark and the power went off so we were left completely in darkness and unable to identify our own employees.

They then used the workers as a shield so that they could all come inside the house and they were downstairs chanting and singing and making threats. They sent one of the workers upstairs to demand the shotgun from me to take back to them. I refused and this employee stayed upstairs with us. They then grabbed his son who was downstairs and from what I could gather they threatened to either kill or injure him if he didn't go back downstairs with the weapon. He went back downstairs but without the weapon. After about five minutes they told all the singing workers to go upstairs to use them as a shield once more. My wife was standing at the top of the stairs with a can of mace and we were trying to identify the workers one by one as they came up the stairs, as. After about 15 workers came through, she could not identify someone and so she sprayed him and he ran back downstairs and out of the house.

This incensed the thugs and they proceeded to break down the back door and started building a fire in the downstairs lounge directly below us. As we have a wooden floor upstairs this posed a great threat and we thought we would be burnt alive, which is when I said that we would come out and asked if they would let us leave peacefully which they agreed to do. We asked the ring-leader to identify himself. We came downstairs and he demanded the shotgun from me which was loaded and off safety but I refused. They then insisted that I give it to them and I began to unload it and they attacked me. They then grabbed my wife around the throat and she started screaming. While they were trying to take the shotgun from me three shots went off outside the house into the ground as it is a semi-automatic shotgun. They then took the shotgun from me and wrestled me to the ground and started beating me with what I assume was sticks, or pipes and kicking me with their boots. They dragged my wife outside and they were trying to strangle her. At this stage she managed to bite the hand of the man who was grabbing her round the throat. Whereupon he started to beat her. At one time there were at least four men beating and kicking her.

They then tied me up with rope and threw me into the back of their pick-up.

My wife was also being beaten. When they had finished with her, one of them grabbed her by her feet and dragged her over to the vehicle. They then demanded that she stand up and get into the back of

156

the truck which she was unable to do. One of them grabbed her by the hair, pulled her into a standing position and pushed her up against the back of the truck and told her to get in, which she did. They searched her and found our car-keys in her pocket and demanded she show them which vehicle they were for, so then they drove the car onto the lawn and parked near the truck where I was tied up.

When the immobilizer for the vehicle went off they demanded my wife show them the immobilizer switch. One of them then drove off with the vehicle which we never saw again. They still had all the employees on the lawn around a fire that had been lit by the front door and they were being forced to sing.

There were about four or five of them around the vehicle watching the two of us and all the time screaming abuse and threatening to kill either one or both of us and also speaking about how they would do it. This must have gone on for almost an hour, all the while burning my feet with cigarettes.

We saw vehicle lights shining towards us and then my wife was told to get out of the vehicle and was dragged towards the headlights of the vehicle that had arrived. When she got to the vehicle she saw there were four armed policeman from Kadoma Police Station who asked what had happened. She told them briefly and demanded that they fetch me immediately from the vehicle as she feared for my life. One of the thugs came and untied me and told me to get out of the vehicle and made me walk towards the headlights of the parked vehicle. I noticed that they were armed policeman. The incident was described in more detail to them and they accompanied us into the house to get some warm clothing. Once we were in the house we saw that the gun cabinet had been opened and ransacked and that my weapons were missing. I informed them. They then took us out of the house and told us to get in their vehicle as we were going to Chegutu Police Station to make a report.

We got to Chegutu Police Station and they had to call some superior officer to take a statement and he only arrived as we were leaving to go to Harare to get urgent medical attention. No policeman of any authority seemed to show any interest in taking our statements.

At the Avenues Clinic in the city many x-rays and CT scans were taken

My injuries were two cracked vertebrae in my lower back, fractured cheekbone, fractured nose with copious bleeding into my sinuses, and extensive lacerations and deep-tissue bruising to my face and back and a bite on my right earlobe.

My wife's injuries were fractured cheekbones, fractures around the orbital socket round one eye, perforated eardrum, cracked ribs and extensive bruising to her face and back and throat.

The Elephant and the Marabou
David Brooke Mee

We drove the 360km from Harare to Kariba and parked at Andora Harbour where Peter's boat, fully fuelled, was waiting for us, then carried our supplies – enough for four days – down the slipway and we stowed them. It didn't take us long, and within an hour we were under way, heading across the lake to the southern side and the Ume River.

The water up the river was high but murky because of recent heavy rains. Sometimes a lot of rain helps the fishing, particularly after the dry season when insects, spiders, worms, slugs and small mammals get washed into the rivers causing the fish to go into a feeding frenzy, indiscriminately snapping at anything that floats past them. Sometimes it's not so helpful though, because the silt makes the water murky and the fish don't see your bait. We didn't know what to expect.

We slowly made our way up-stream, hugging the left bank and trying our luck at all sorts of things but mainly bream and tiger fish. We'd chug slowly along, keeping our eyes open for a likely spot, then kill the motor and drift up to a dead Mopane tree where I, sitting at the bow, would tie up. Each time the motor sputtered into silence I was struck by a sense of stillness and tranquillity, accentuated by the *slap slap slap* of water against the fibre-glass hull. While I waited for the fish,

159

which had been scared off by the boat approaching, to return, I'd sit in the warmth of the sun and listen for those familiar sounds that heighten the sensation of being one with this wilderness. The *uh uh uh* of a bull hippo warning rivals to stay away from his territory, or the mournful haunting cry of the fish eagle, were as common out there as the sounds of yapping dogs in the suburbs of Harare, but much more comforting. The bark of a baboon in the hills would sometimes carry clearly across the water, but always the unceasingly sound of birds, near and far, their cries both loud and soft, intermingled in a heavenly chorus.

The fishing was bad. The water was too murky and we'd arrived too late after the rains, so the fish were engorged as well as blind. We didn't mind though, simply being out there enjoying each other's company and the serenity of our surroundings was enough. The situation did not improve at all on the opposite bank when, after two days, we turned around and started making our way back towards the mouth of the river and the open water, but we were catching enough bream each day for our evening meal so we were content. Each night we would make our way into a bay and either tie up to a tree and float, or pull the boat on shore and spend the night aground. When we were settled we'd cook whatever fish we'd caught that day and fall asleep to the sound of the African night coming alive.

So it was that in the late afternoon of our last day we found our way into a huge bay surrounded by low hills on three sides and sheltered by a large island to our east. The river had been quite choppy all day but as we entered the bay we were all struck by the contrasting calm. The water was so still its surface was like a mirror and it was clear and inviting, so we killed the motor and drifted while we took turns lowering ourselves off the back of the boat into the cool water, then standing on the transom and soaping ourselves down to wash off the filth of the past few days.

After I'd bathed I put on a clean pair of shorts and went to sit once again at the bow, relishing the way the slight breeze cooled my wet skin and giving me goose bumps. We pushed our way through a mat of water hyacinth, through the shallows beyond and beached on a short strip of sand beneath a large grassy mound where I jumped to the shore to tie the rope to a big, half-buried log. I was done with fishing.

I made myself comfortable on the bow of the boat and contented myself with basking in the serenity of the setting. Pete and Gary fetched themselves a drink from the cold box, lit up some smokes and settled themselves on the back of the boat to cast into the peaceful waters and talk quietly.

Nothing stirred the surface, except rather ironically, fish jumping out of the water way out of casting distance as if to mock our earlier failed attempts to catch them, and the occasional, very light puff of a breeze that succeeded in creating a tiny ripple.

I watched a Marabou Stork walking slowly up and down the length of the shore on the other side of the bay. He reminded me of an elderly gentleman strolling

161

along a beach with his hands in his pockets, stopping occasionally to bend down and look at something on the ground in front of him, then looking up and solemnly resuming the careful measured steps of his mission.

A whisper of something inexplicable caused me to look over my shoulder at the shore, and to my astonishment I saw an elephant cow standing on the crest of the hill not more than twenty metres away. I shouldn't have been taken aback considering we were invaders in her world, but the sight of her so close took me by surprise. I held my breath as I watched her lift her trunk and move the flared tip to sniff the air before taking a step and starting down the hill towards me. Because Gary and Pete had talked all the time I knew the elephant was aware of our presence and I knew she wouldn't be alarmed when I quietly said, "Hey guys, look at this".

They reeled in their lines, ready for a hasty departure if necessary, and the three of us sat quietly watching as this matriarch drew closer and closer and, without hesitating, stepped deliberately over the thick nylon rope I'd tied to the log half an hour before. At that point she was no more than ten metres away, close enough for me to smell the dust on her warm body and to count the individual lashes on her one visible eye. She continued for a few more metres then stopped and emitted a low rumble before moving on her way.

Moments later another elephant appeared and, without hesitating, followed the path taken by the matriarch, then another and another until, all told, six elephants, comprising four females and two youngsters (one of them very small) had silently walked past us and made their way to the far side of the bay, followed by an entourage of egrets. The stork, seemingly put out by the intrusion on his privacy, took to the air and flapped away.

None of us had been lucky enough to be close enough to wild elephants in similar circumstances before, so we chatted casually about it and all agreed that it had been a magical moment. Pete and Gary returned to their fishing and I lay back and watched the elephants bathe before peeling away heading off, one at a time, into the trees at the top of the slope.

The larger of the two baby elephants had different ideas though. He told his mother he wasn't ready to go yet; he wanted to hang out for a little while longer and he told his mother that he was big enough to look after himself. *"You head on alone"* he said, *"and I'll catch up with you later – when it suits me"*.

So off she went and within no time at all her massive grey body disappeared into the dense foliage, and the youngster, clearly a little more nervous than he was ready to admit, was left all alone on the shore.

As the small herd was starting to withdraw, old man Marabou reappeared. He was high up, riding thermals, doing big wide circles, biding his time till peace and quiet returned to his tiny fiefdom. He circled a few more times after mother had left, getting lower and lower with every circuit, waiting for the youngster to leave too, but when it became clear that he wasn't going to, he quietly landed, put his hands in his pockets and resumed his sombre plodding.

The little elephant wasn't paying attention to the stork; he was too focused on interesting things in his immediate vicinity; a stick here, a clump of grass there, a swish of dust or a sip of water and, all the time he was distracted, the Marabou plodded closer and closer, minding his own business and just getting on with the serious business of being a scavenger.

Old man Marabou was perhaps three feet behind the little elephant and was just leaning forward to pick something up in his beak when the little fellow turned around and saw him. He got such a fright that he screamed in alarm whilst the old undertaker was in turn sufficiently startled to squawk and flap into the air then land and rattle his bill angrily at the little chap.

The display caused all three of us on the boat to burst out laughing, but we stopped laughing immediately when mother, who'd obviously been waiting just below the ridge of the hill, (far enough away to give the little guy a sense of being alone but near enough to be useful in a crisis) burst out of the foliage on *tip-toes* and with her ears spread wide to signal her readiness to fight for her *little boy* if necessary. She had, naturally I suppose, assumed that it had been us who had caused her youngster's distress.

Fortunately her large brain very quickly took in all the facts as she came racing out of the bush and she could tell immediately that we were too far away to have posed any kind of threat. On the other hand, old man

Marabou was still rattling his bill with indignation so she knew the scream had been a false alarm. She stopped her charge and turned towards her lad, who was now as embarrassed as a youngster can be when making a fool of himself, but she didn't laugh at him or scold him; she reached out her trunk and rested it over his shoulder as if to say, "there there, it's OK. You're a brave lad".

Then they walked together up the slope and disappeared silently into the bush.

Fall Guy
Brian Sherry

I was appointed as the first resident Wildlife Research Officer in the Gonarezhou National Park in the south-east Lowveld in late 1969, and I was closely involved in the monitoring and management of the park's elephant populations. This included aerial and ground surveys and broad assessment of habitat damage due to elephant numbers. I provided much of the formal evidence of 'over-population', as well as recommendations for management solutions. These included not only culling but also provision of water supplies to extend the elephants' dry-season range, and removal of tsetse control fencing which was restricting elephant movement within the park.

When it came to culling – the controlled removal of excessive numbers of elephants (literally thousands over a five-year period) - I also played a major part in the process on the ground, leading the Research Team in collecting biological data from the animals killed.

At times I also took part in locating target herds from the air and in the actual shooting of the elephants. As part of the reduction in elephant numbers, staff from both Field and Research Branches also engaged in the *ad hoc* destruction of fence-breaking and crop-raiding elephants over the years. I was comfortable with this destruction, mainly of bulls, as a means of trying to

166

redress the inequality in the male/female ratio created by removing family groups just of cows and calves during the main culling programmes.

During 1976, following independence in Mozambique and the escalation of the Rhodesian Bush War, it became more and more difficult to manage the park. We were very much on the front-line and largely on a care-and-maintenance basis.

At the same time there was ever increasing activity by the Armed Forces in the area.

Added to all that, I was not getting on well with the Department. An altercation between Research and Field developed and Head Office decided to transfer me out of Gonarezhou; but not before I was drawn into an intrigue that landed me in jail.

To lay the story to rest I now tell it in most of its extraordinary detail. If I miss anything out you can blame my memory, or maybe that at the time I was just a bit 'bush-happy'. Surely something strange was happening in my head, for I remember one night in my isolated house on the river bank at Chipinda Pools soon after my wife had left me, asleep alone behind the security fence, the sand-bags and the bullet-proof window screening, I woke myself up firing my revolver through the bedroom door.

In those closing days of Rhodesia I had become friendly with a man called Jannie Meyer and we had done some hunting together, both on Buffalo Range Ranch where he ran the Game Section, and on the Mkwasine. Jannie was also a Selous Scout. He badly

167

wanted to get some experience of elephant hunting and he repeatedly asked me if it could be arranged in the Gonarezhou. I had told him the truth – first he would need to become an attested Honorary Officer of the Department, something I could not arrange myself. It would have to be done through the Field Branch and Head Office.

But nothing came of that idea.

About this time there were rumblings in the conservation world about escalating elephant poaching in and around the Gonarezhou, and little bits of evidence and hearsay began to emerge.

The Armed Forces were at the centre of these rumours; both the regular Army and the Selous Scouts, and links were suggested between the Army and some of the Department's Field staff. Rumours said illegal hunting was rife in all areas: the Chuanja Hills in the north, the Nyamasikana Basin and the Border Corridor in the centre, extending beyond Mabalauta to Chikwarakwara in the south.

At the time I most certainly was not involved in any unofficial hunting or killing of elephant myself.

But this was to change.

Around mid-1976 Jannie approached me again with the news that a Police Special Branch Officer had been posted to Buffalo Range to investigate these rumours. Would I be prepared to meet him?

Well, no harm in that I thought. Go ahead.

In the meeting with *SB,* who I am not sure why but I am still reluctant to name, he outlined a simple strategy.

He was going to set himself up as a poacher, and for this he needed some unmarked elephant bull ivory which he could use to establish his criminal credentials and to back up his claim to be able to supply ivory.

He also told me he wanted to become familiar with at least part of the Gonarezhou, and shoot a few bull elephants himself, to provide *bona fide* experience of elephant hunting. With that experience and the ivory, he thought he could work his way into any network he might uncover.

My first reaction was to tell him I did not have the authority to do what he asked, but there was a problem holding me back. If, as was suspected, there were some people in the Department who were involved in the illegal hunting, any approach at however high a level could filter down and blow the operation, which I believed to be bona fide.

The question of unmarked ivory was a difficult issue but one I could get round: standard procedure was that tusks arriving at the Station were automatically stamped, recorded and locked in an inaccessible strong room; once they were in, I could not take them out. But since I was the only one involved, I could get away without putting them in.

What if we were found out?

I was assured that in spite of the risks, all this had been covered with the local Police. By way of fidelity, I was given the name of a Police Officer I should call for in the event of questions being asked. I knew the man they named, so I was easily gulled into believing that

169

there was a greater interest here than just the Department's way of doing things. There was no mention of any personal financial returns at this stage; to me that was something I had not even thought of.

I was drawn in.

So the three of us went off on a couple of sorties into the Gonarezhou in *SB's* Police Land Rover. The cover story was a simple '*Special Branch work*'. There could be no question about our credentials – a Special Branch Officer travelling with a Selous Scout (Jannie) and a member of the park's staff (myself) in a Police vehicle operating in a forward military operational area seemed convincing. It was to me.

One of these sorties was genuine enough to add to my sense of security – we had to drop-off a Special Branch informer somewhere along the internal fence of the Border Corridor with Mozambique. He was on his way to infiltrate one of the terrorist camps in Mozambique.

And so it was that in due course *SB* got the elephant hunting experience he wanted, shooting two bulls in different locations, on two different occasions, and some unmarked ivory. He asked me to take a few photos of him with the elephants; I should have smelt a rat when he insisted it should not be with my own camera.

Then he asked for a regular stream of ivory to drip-feed into a market he had been able to penetrate.

I made a few more trips into the park just with Jannie, and we added a few more pairs of tusks to *SB's* ivory stream. I also made a few sorties on my own, the ivory also all going to him.

170

It wasn't easy. Although exciting, it was hard work, stalking and killing elephant bulls in thick bush completely alone, and returning later to the carcasses, to pull the tusks and carry them back to the Land Rover. And all the time with the chance of an encounter with terrorists in this forward operational area. I had nothing to worry about from our own National Parks patrols – there weren't any.

In hind-sight I find it difficult to believe that I should have been so foolhardy as to carry out these solo hunts. On one occasion I shot an adult bull in thick bush at very close quarters. He dropped with a clean brain shot, but his companion charged without hesitation and I had to put him down at even closer range. The stopping power of the .458 was comforting.

SB soon told me that he had traced an outlet 'over the border' in South Africa, possibly already receiving ivory from our area. He said that with his position and connections he was able to move freely across the border at Beitbridge in his Police Land Rover without being searched. He then offered me some compensation for the risks I was taking. I reminded him that this was not what I was in it for, but he insisted and I accepted.

It was downhill for me from there on.

Up to this point I could justify what I was doing. Accepting payment pushed me over the top and I knew that I had been eased into common criminality. But by then there was no simple way out. I had been well and truly trapped.

It didn't take long after that before I began to know for sure that I was being watched. On one occasion I saw the Senior Ranger's Piper Cub overhead, obviously keeping me under surveillance; on another, a government Land Rover pulled away ahead of me, waiting for me as I was returning from a solo elephant hunt in the hills in the late afternoon; and then my house was broken into and searched in my absence.

It all added up, but still I felt that I was taking part in police business and that my only guilt was in accepting money for it.

And so the slope became increasingly slippery over a couple of months, until one morning in February 1977 I was approached by a Police Officer and his Constable while shopping in Chiredzi. They invited me to go with them to the Police Station to answer some questions about elephant hunting in the Gonrezhou. Incredibly, the interrogating officer turned out to be none other than the man named by *SB* as the one to quote if ever I was questioned!

At Parks HQ there was mixed reaction to my arrest. The Director's view was that if I had broken the law I should face the charges in court. The Chief Research Officer suggested that as I was legally entitled to kill elephants in the Gonarezhou I should simply be discharged for misconduct.

My own state of mind at this stage was such that I didn't much care. Still, it was very much against my better judgement that I accepted my lawyer's advice to

172

plead guilty when at last I was charged, and to say nothing to implicate others.

They already knew about Jannie, and he was charged with illegal hunting, but 'SB' melted into the background and was never seen or heard of again.

The lawyer's argument was that a guilty plea would keep the case short and end with nothing more than a hefty fine. I went along with this advice. But what a surprise was in store for me. And for most everyone else watching.

I was sentenced to 18 months in jail.

Small compensation, but by way of acknowledging he'd got it all wrong, the lawyer waived his fee.

On my own advice I quickly decided not to appeal. There didn't seem much point and anyway I couldn't afford it. What I'd done in accepting money, albeit no more than a few hundred dollars, made everything else stupid and wrong. That I was the victim of a well-laid criminal scheme was ultimately not acceptable vindication. I have never overcome a sense of shame that effectively I did not tell 'the whole truth' in court, and subsequently I was branded as having killed those elephants out of greed.

Perhaps worse still, was the irony that my own actions had drawn the focus away from, and effectively protected the real villains who killed so many more of those Lowveld elephants in the first place.

Khami prison might not have been as bad in those days as it was to become later, but it was no doddle at first.

173

Before Khami I spent about two weeks in solitary confinement in Buffalo Range Prison while waiting to give evidence in Jannie's trial. I was treated pretty well.

Then, after Jannie was similarly convicted, the dreaded journey to Khami.

...

The good news was that half my sentence was suspended. And I soon learnt that, with good conduct while locked up, I might be eligible for up to three months remission. I also discovered that there were good people who knew I had been shafted and would do what they could to help. The new Chief Research Officer at Parks was one of them, and he arranged for me to be able to write up some valuable research work, ironically on elephants, while in jail.

Not long after arriving at Khami I was given 'A Class' status, and assigned to work on the prison farm dairy. I was also given office space, and there it was that I completed my paper on '*The Growth of Elephants in the Gonarezhou*', which was published in the South African Journal of Wildlife Research.

After six months I was released on full remission for good conduct. Free at last to pick up the pieces of my shattered life and head for a fresh start.

Que Que's Lady Steptoe
*Researched, compiled and nailed together by a posse
of her grandchildren*

Que Que was once one of the richest towns in Rhodesia – busy and rich because of the gold mines that sprang up there. The richest of those was, of course, the Globe and Phoenix, but there were many others too. There is a stretch of the main road through Que Que that still honours this fact. It is called 'The Golden Mile'.

And with the prosperity there was a flourishing white community. People came from many parts of the world looking for work on the mines. One of them was a Scot called John Mathieson Beaton, and he arrived there from Johannesburg with his young German bride when the country called Rhodesia was barely twenty years old.

In due course the couple produced a daughter and three sons, but it seems the marriage was not a happy one. Judging by her subsequent career and life choices, one could most reasonably draw the conclusion that she was a hard and determined woman of fixed ideas who must have been extremely difficult to live with.

The details of what happened in the early years of their life together have been lost in the swirling mists of uncaring time, but at some stage when the children were still young the husband disappeared from the story, died or just departed, and his German wife was

175

left to find a way to bring up her brood in a land far from her own, still learning to speak a language she found difficult, and among people she thought cold and unfriendly. To compound her misery, her little girl Elsie then died of accidental poisoning – she had found an enticing blue bottle, emptied the contents into her mouth, and swallowed what proved to be a fatal dose.

In her misery and need, Mrs. Frieda Beaton looked about her for some clue, some opportunity that would keep her and her reduced brood alive. And the thing that most focussed her attention was the amount of waste that surrounded everyone in this affluent environment; good furniture thrown out to make way for newer and flashier gear; car tyres dumped with many more miles of life in them; curtains, pots, pans, clothing, leather belts, horse saddles and harness tackle. Wherever her eye fell it seemed there was useful stuff being discarded without a backward glance. Surely, she thought, there must be people who would pay something for all of this? And she was right.

At first she walked the little town of Que Que herself, knocking on doors and asking the same simple question: "Any old junk you want to get rid of? I can pay."

With the proceeds of her first few collections she bought, or had made, a hand cart which she pushed around the little town almost proudly. As the boys grew big enough they too had to take turns pushing the cart around town, looking for anything their mother could turn to value. Collections multiplied, and she soon found

176

herself the owner of a busy scrap yard. Her canny trader's wit and tough Teutonic hide served her well, and the business flourished. Not that anyone in Que Que knew it. She was far too smart to put her growing wealth on parade in such a small town. Instinctively she knew that part of her success came from a sense of pity in the community; pity and admiration. The good people of Que Que felt sorry for the little *Frau* and they admired her efforts at self-preservation. If they knew how well she was doing, she feared they might switch off.

In any case she had a secret need for money in addition to that of providing for her Rhodesian family. She had a younger brother called Max, blind from birth. Sometime after her marriage her parents had died and Max was now all alone in Germany in the town of Sax Coburg. He was being cared for in a little institution there, a home for the blind. She kept in touch with Max by regular letters to the people caring for him. And from time to time she sent them as much money as she could spare – to buy him little luxuries and improve the quality of his sightless life.

After some years Frieda decided that Que Que was too small for her and she moved to the metropolis of Bulawayo. There she bought a stand on the corner of a busy city street and set up as a trader of all things second hand. The business model must have been a good one, for it was not long before old Ma Beaton owned the entire block. By the time she died she owned more than one; in truth she had become very wealthy indeed. All of that lay far in the future, however, there were still three boys to bring up and educate.

Of course they did not go to the best schools Bulawayo had to offer, and of course they were made to continue working for the business, but surrounded as they were by other young people busy growing up in the wonderful environment of a new country, they inevitably grew up as Rhodesians – tough and independent, keen on sports, keen campers, and generally loving the great outdoors. Of the politics of the time there is no reason to believe they were any different from the masses of other young white men and women then trying to make their way in the life of the new land, they were blissfully unaware of the racial storm brewing for the far distant future. They were also blissfully unaware of another subject that would later on affect them: Frieda was fanatically loyal to her motherland, and she read with growing pride every issue of any newspaper or magazine she could find with stories and reports of the rise of Adolf Hitler and Nazi Germany.

Not much of what she said to her children on the subject has been passed on, but it is known that she reacted with fury when, on the outbreak of world war, all three of her sons volunteered to join the Rhodesian forces and fight *against* Germany.

With her sons away from home and fighting for the 'wrong' side, old Ma Beaton became, to all intents and purposes, free of all family connections, and she worked harder and harder, amassing in time a veritable fortune, none of which she could send, as she would have preferred, to help her brother or her motherland. And although she had no way of knowing it at the time, the blind Max had passed away while the war was still raging.

Ralph, known as Bob, one of her sons, was invalided out of the Rhodesian Air force then serving in Italy, and returned to Bulawayo. He recalled that while recuperating at home there his mother said to him one day "wonderful news about the new bomb, eh Bobby!" She was referring to Germany's new V2, then thought to be a potential game changer for Hitler at a time when things were rapidly going downhill for him.

When the war was finally over, the young Beaton men were not surprised to find themselves unwelcome strangers in their mother's home. Sulking about the surrender of her precious homeland, she shut them off and shut them out. What they thought about it no one now knows. Most likely they assumed she would come out of it. They were young, glad to be alive, excited to be re-kindling careers of their own, and well enough off from their saved service pay not to be dependent on the old lady.

But she never did come out of it. Eventually, with her own eyesight beginning to fail, she sold everything, moved away from them, and went to settle in Cape Town.

When she died in the early sixties the sons were left out of her will. Everything was to go to the blind home that had been the late Max's sanctuary for so long. That part of the will read: "for reasons well known to them I do hereby specifically disinherit my sons..........."

And indeed, they got nothing of the vast estate.

Ironically, neither did Max's sanctuary.

The liquidators tidied up, and all the proceeds went to probate in South Africa, pending transfer to the beneficiary in Sax Coburg. But that part of Germany was then in communist East Germany and the South Africa government declined to allow transfer of the inheritance. Instead, the money lay in a trust fund for many more years, no doubt providing a lucrative source of regular work for the lawyers, and with inflation, simply wasting away in value.

Eventually, when a new generation of the old lady's descendants started looking into the business with some hope of reviving their family claims to the cash, the fund was suddenly closed and what was left of it went to another randomly chosen home for blind people in West Germany.

One Old Woman Writes
Sue

I am a 70 year old white widow living in Zimbabwe. My husband died in May this year and apart from the house, I was left destitute because his only child, from a previous marriage, did not want to share any inheritance. Suffice to say, I had no option but to survive and the only way I could do so was to sell my furniture, jewellery and anything else I had, just to earn some valuable US$. With careful economising, painting, and selling my work, growing my own vegetables and limiting myself to one meal a day, I've kept going. I am luckier than most, but only because I still have the ability to 'make a plan'. I couldn't afford a dentist, so I pulled out my own teeth. I couldn't afford a doctor, so I stitched a dog's bite on my arm with needle and thread.

I look after an African family who have nothing – all seven of them – trying to ensure that they get food and whatever else I can find to keep them going. I have a young white family living in a cottage with their two babies, and a young bachelor living in a thatched hut, whose salary doesn't even cover his basic needs and together we form a 'family', looking out for each other and doing the best we can to keep going.

The only thing I have plenty of is loneliness and spare time, and I have put out feelers to try and join some Non-Government Organisations to go to the rural areas to help with the cholera epidemic. I am not a qualified

181

nurse – but I care deeply and I know how desperate the situation is, but have not had any luck, because possibly they think me too old. But I am not! My whole life has been directed towards looking after disabled servicemen, orphans, and now the indigenous folk of this country. There are those of us who are fighting not only for our own lives, but for those of our countrymen. The fancy cars seen on the roads today belong to Government personnel and Party officials who live in luxury.

I heard of two elderly white people who lived in a disused shed. They used to own a house and a car, but found themselves with nothing when they had their land and home stolen. A kind African let them live in a shed on his property. On their wedding anniversary the wife went out and sold her wedding ring. She and her husband decided they would have one last night out on the 'town' so they went to a hotel and had a great dinner and shared a glass of the wine they had left over from their night out, curled up into their blankets on the stone floor, and died. They had poisoned themselves and were found holding each other in their arms as they couldn't bear to suffer another day.

Every story is different. I am still here and refuse to let go. There are too many people left in this country who need compassion, care and hope to go on. Although there are organisations and charitable groups who try to help, there aren't enough of them. But the solution lies with all of us here – black, white and coloured, to start caring for each other. It takes more than courage, it

182

takes fury and grief to explode into action. I have taken in people who have had their families murdered in cold blood, and experienced such fear you cannot imagine the enormity of it. I have sat up through the nights watching the house and listening for intruders. There are so few of us left now – maybe 2000?

Today, I ventured into Harare city, and I saw a populace of 'stick figures' robotically going about their business, faces closed and dull. Starvation, AIDS, cholera, anthrax and extreme poverty have robbed them of all hope. It was not all those years ago we saw glossy fat women with their babies. Today, I did not even see one baby on the back of a mother. The High Court was empty. No staff, so I could not get on with the Estate of my late husband, but that no longer seems so important.

Everywhere we see the portrait of Robert Mugabe in every government building, but nobody looks at it much anymore. Fly speckled and faded from the sun, he just hangs there as a reminder of the horrors he can impose. I live not far from his residence, Government House, and in the past we could hear the screaming sirens of his cavalcade proclaiming 'the master' is in our presence. Today, there is no fanfare, just secrecy of his journeys, because he is afraid – good! We've all been afraid for too damn long. Our fear has persisted as babies, children, men and women are murdered.

I have no intention of leaving this land in which I was born. I belong here as much as my darker skinned countrymen. I love this country, and the people who inhabit it. And that is why I am a proud Zimbabwean.

Every day we receive a small gift – be it a couple of tomatoes from someone's garden, or a small bunch of wild flowers, and that's Christmas. We are poor – but we are richer in other senses nobody can understand unless they go through the torments this country has faced over these last many years. We yearn for light at the end of the tunnel, but refuse to pick up arms and kill others as we have been killed. We wait for justice, not from them, but from a Power beyond our capacity. It will come!

To all those who live elsewhere and who have never experienced the deprivation that just one man can dole out to millions, let me tell you it is a testing experience. There are many here who do what they can to make the 'oldies' leave this vicious world feeling loved, regardless of their colour.

This is just my story. Multiply it a thousand times – and include the human greed that makes it harder for us to withstand the hardships, but which is prevalent in all humanity regardless of race and creed. Above all, learn from it, because but for the Grace of God there goes you.

With warmth, from an old white Zimbabwean woman.

Ramping Grey with Patrick
Patti North
From *Last of the Rhodesians (Facebook 2017)*

Patrick owned a Mini when my sister and I were still at school. He was "cool", mainly because he was older and had a car and a driver's licence. Some called him a cowboy.

Patrick would come and ask if Penni and I could go for a ride down town to the Eskimo Hut for an ice cream with him. After the usual "be-careful/I'll-hang-draw-and-quarter-you-if-anything-happens-to-the-twins" from my old man, we would set off on our joyride.

Leaving 8 Fife Street, North end side, we would travel at a moderate pace in case the folk were watching, take a left at Queen's Sports Club, then a right into Grey Street heading for the Eskimo Hut.

With its deep wide dips for the storm drains that were at all intersections you remember, Bulawayo was just made to be ramped, and Patrick would instantly become a street cowboy, egged on by the two of us – *faster.. faster... go faster*! And Grey Street seemed endless in those days.

How that little Mini flew.

I swear we were airborne... and even though the undercarriage of the Mini must have been taking a beating, we just seemed to go on and on. To us "ramping" down Grey Street was the most thrilling adventure of all. We arrived at the Eskimo Hut, totally wind-blown and mind-blown too.

After enjoying the Eskimo Hut's wickedly delicious *Choc 99* - ice cream cone with a Chocolate Flake in it - we would head back home, once again ramping Grey Street. We had the time of our lives, then try to calm ourselves down, running our fingers through our hair and smiling from ear to ear.

Patrick would drive slowly into our half-moon drive and with his dashing smile, say "Thank you Mr Grieve – the girls are back safely"

Tickey
Edie Hawkins

I know Tickey had another name, it would have been written down on that strange identity document all black men had to have back then, but as I never actually saw his 'stupa', I never thought of him any other way. I do know he came from Malawi, but he had been away for so many years that he had ceased to think of it as home, and he never went back there to visit family on any of his many periods of long leave.

He was our 'house boy' when I was young, and we all loved him dearly. We lived on a farm near Gatooma. Tickey was very much a member of the family, and although the word 'boy' has been made to sound unpleasantly paternalistic and even pejorative, in those days it was nothing of the kind. If you had asked Tickey what his job was, he would have answered without thinking, without any shame, and more probably with some pride, 'houseboy!' Domestic servants earned more than common labourers and they felt decidedly superior.

There are people these days who believe we should no longer use words that have been made offensive by time and politics, and that sits alright with me. I no longer have a houseboy or a garden boy, but if I did I would be sure to refer to them by some more appropriate title, but to shy away from words we used then is a perversion of history. Worse than that, it implies that we should feel ashamed for the way we were, and to that I can only say "aikona, handidi, no thank you".

Tickey was tall and rangy, loose limbed, athletic and super energetic. He was also clean and tidy, always giving the impression in his crisp khaki shorts and shirt that he had only seconds before come out of the shower to put them on. He was profoundly happy to be doing what he did. I cannot remember a single occasion when Tickey had to be corrected, or even instructed what to do. From top to bottom he cleaned the house each day, making up the beds, sweeping floors, dusting surfaces and generally keeping things spotless. Once a week he changed bed linen, polished the floors and cleaned the windows. He was also solely responsible for the laundry and ironing. His was a heavy load, but a load that he carried with ease and appeared to enjoy, until that is, his fate caught up with him.

It was some years after I had grown up and left home, and the actual incident happened one Christmas time when I was visiting the farm with my husband and our own small family.

It was in the morning of the day before Christmas when most of us were on the veranda of my brother's home, a few hundred yards away from my parents' house on a little hill where Tickey was supposedly relaxing. He had been left drinking tea in the kitchen up there, and he was supposed to be 'knocking off' for the holidays. Instead he chose to give the old people's dining room one last going over, and he was on his knees with brush and polish when he looked into the eyes of a deadly black mamba, a ten-foot long example of Africa's most awesome snake.

A single bite from a black mamba has been known to kill a man in less than five minutes. It is an angry and aggressive beast that will usually go headlong onto the attack rather than scoot and slither away as most other snakes would always rather do when they meet the potential trouble of people.

Tickey was frozen. Sheer terror, or perhaps instinct, saved him, for he did not move a muscle, not even to focus his eyes on the dreadful head so close to his own.

Trying to recall the experience later, he told us he was looking at the wall beyond the snake and that the head itself was merely a blur before him. He demonstrated how close it was – two hands, less than a forearm's length.

How long this wall-staring state of shock and horror lasted he could not say beyond the fact that it seemed like his whole life.

Eventually the mamba surrendered, doubling back on itself and retreating to the far corner of the room under the sideboard.

Only when he saw the last few inches of the tail disappearing under the gap did Tickey make a move. But then it was a quick one, involving every muscle in his body, including those around the larynx. He ran screaming from the house and down the little hill towards where we were all gathered. We heard him coming and were already all up on our feet and rushing to the front door when he appeared, still screaming, "Mamba! Mamba! Mamba!"

At length he calmed down a bit, enough to blurt out what had happened and to communicate the fact that the snake must still be in the house. While my brother went off to deal with it, the rest of us stayed behind to attend to Tickey, to comfort him and assure him that he was not the worse thought of for his terror and panic. He was quite grey with fright shock, and he said nothing more, merely standing there and shaking his head slowly as if in utter disbelief.

We heard a shot, and shortly afterwards my brother appeared with the dead mamba. He laid it on the ground for all to see. It measured ten feet and a few inches with a maximum girth of about three or four inches. Even in death it seemed fatally threatening, and we were all relieved when it was thrown onto the fire that blazed away beneath a metal drum water boiler behind the kitchen.

What should have been the end of the story was just the beginning for Tickey. Nothing anyone said could shake him of the conviction that the mamba had been 'sent' to kill him. His good nature dissolved, his appearance began to show the signs of a fatal obsession. No longer was he the happy conscientious man he had been before. Now he shuffled through his work each day, stopping every few minutes to mutter something to himself and shake his head sadly.

The old folks were at first kind and understanding towards him, but as the days became weeks with no change, Dad felt he had to have a talk with Tickey. He tried to explain that what had happened could have happened at any time and to anybody living in rural Rhodesia of that time. All snakes were common, mambas slightly less so but still quite plentiful. Over the years on that farm the family had lost at least three dogs to the bite of mambas, and sightings were a regular occurrence. But Tickey remained unplacated, shaking his head to all explanations and simply repeating what had become his mantra, 'umtaggart', meaning a curse, or sorcerer's spell; someone, for some unknown reason hated him and through some powerful wizard had sent the snake to kill him.

Dad asked him if there was anything he could do to neutralise the spell and make it go away, to which his only answer was "I doubt."

Later on though, it may have been two months or more, when he had really begun to look haggard and very ill, he asked to borrow money – quite a sum – to visit a local witch doctor and try to buy his way clear of whatever it was that had been laid upon him. The old man readily agreed, and arranged for the money and a month's leave for Tickey to attend to the business. Once again I was on the farm on the day Tickey was leaving, and he came to say goodbye to the family. To my eyes he was a dreadful sight, looking much like a man dying from some awful wasting disease. But he managed a cheerful goodbye and said he would be back as soon as he could be – when "all of this" he said gesturing towards his tattered state, was over. He asked Dad to

191

look after his wife and two children, and then he left, carrying only a small suitcase.

We did not see him again.

From time to time word reached the farm that Tickey needed money to visit another witchdoctor, and arrangements were cheerfully made. After about six months however, there was no further communication, and we eventually heard only that Tickey had died in his home country of Malawi. He was, according to our calculations, 45 years-old at most.

Naturally the story got round. All the workers on the family farm knew of it in intimate detail, but it went further afield, much further afield.

Something like two years later my brother went one weekend to play golf in Mutare, more than a hundred miles away from home. Milling around on the first tee while waiting for the game to get under way, he was chatting to the young caddy who had been selected to carry his bag. The caddy asked him where he was from, and when he mentioned Gatooma and the name of his farm, the young man said he knew of the place. In particular he was aware of the sad story of a man called Tickey, who he described as an 'uncle'.

"Do you know what happened to Tickey?" my brother asked, fishing for some new information I suppose.

"They said Mamba," the youngster answered, "but everybody knows it was a wizard."

Nelson my Uitkyk Cock
Marty Weps

For a year or so I lived on a small farm called Uitkyk in the Midlands of Zimbabwe not far from what is now Gweru. I was between jobs, between lives, and between wives, yet happy to be on my own, away from the press of people, with nothing much to do except feed the fowls, of which there were enough to keep several households well supplied with eggs and Sunday roast. The owners of the place were distant relatives, gone to Europe on an emergency family mission, and they wouldn't be back any time soon.

Uitkyk had once been the homestead farm of the Malherbe family, whose roots, I imagine, went all the way back to the arrival in South Africa of the French Huguenots in the late seventeenth century. 'Bad vegetables' I muttered to myself sometimes, mocking their name because the small garden they must have laid out nearly a hundred years ago looked more like a cemetery now, with black rocks marking the borders of all the beds where a handful of sorry looking greens struggled for survival. It was they who had named the farm Uitkyk.

'Uitkyk' is Afrikaans, and it means 'outlook' or view'. But it also could mean 'look out' I suppose, or even 'beware'. Since there was no real view to speak of, what could there possibly have been on that quiet place to be wary of, I wondered? Lions perhaps, or maybe even marauding elephants? In any case that kind of danger was all very much in the past, or was it?

Livingstone, my uncle's gardener, stepped in to put me straight. He told me to be careful of the cock bird in the fowl run. It was, he said, *maningi* cheeky. *Maningi sterek*!

'The hell with that.' I thought, 'how much of a threat can a cock of his size be compared to my 70 kg?' Thus piqued, I went straight into his domain, and found out soon enough that he was indeed, very 'cheeky', repeatedly charging me and hurling his large golden feathered frame, spurs first, at my uncovered legs. The impact wasn't particularly painful, just irritatingly unpleasant, and I retreated. And for some time thereafter I left the egg collecting to Livingstone. But it niggled me.

The cock, meanwhile, had been emboldened by our single encounter, and when my frequent walks around the garden took me anywhere near the fowl run, he would fling himself wildly against the netting in my direction, a very public challenge to further combat. Usually I was bright enough to laugh at this madness, but one Sunday afternoon, inflamed perhaps by a pair of strong lunch-time gins and tonic, I rose to the occasion, and went in like a bullfighter armed only with attitude – no cape, no sword, and no suit of lights.

The low entrance to the chicken run forced me to stoop, and the cock took the opportunity to get in a few early blows, to which I merely responded with a quiet "*Toro, toro.*"

Once free to go full stretch inside the run, however, I prepared myself for a fuller, more two-sided encounter. Who would be the first to chicken out? I settled myself for the expected charge, adopting a stance more like a featherweight boxer than a matador – fists clenched, arms up, shoulders hunched, and knees slightly bent and mobile, ready for anything – attack or defence. I fancied my chances.

"Come on you little squirt," I hissed. "Come on. Let's see what you've got!"

My unexpected aggression seemed to unsettle him a little. The next charge was slower and less angry. I reached out like El Cordobes or any other well-seasoned matador and gently stroked his slightly raised neck feathers to show my complete mastery of the situation. It was a liberty he could not ignore. Enraged once more, he cackled and screamed and hurled himself upon my person, all spurs and feathers and horny flying feet.

I was ready for him, and skipped nimbly out of the way.

As he regained his grip on the ground, he thrust his head angrily towards me, feathers up in full dander. At the same instant I reached out with my open right hand to give him a wristy slap. The combined effect of his thrust and mine could not have been more perfect. I felt the contact right up to my shoulder. It was remarkably solid, and I knew it must have dazed him, but even so I was surprised by the result.

The mighty cock dropped to the ground, pole-axed. There he lay with only an occasional slight muscular

195

twitch that told me he was either already dead or on the point of passing away.

Shocked and somewhat concerned, for I had not meant to do such serious mischief to the old warrior, I gently raised the lid of his skyward eye. Not a sign of life was there to be seen. The lid remained open, the revealed eye staring blindly out at the world he was no longer a part of.

My remorse was instant. How could I have killed such a brave and courageous little beast less than a twenty-fifth my own size and fighting weight? What kind of a drunken bastard had I become?

I stared unhappily a moment longer at the unmoving carcass and then went off to tell the gardener the sad news and ask him to take care of the final details. No doubt he would enjoy a good meal out of the old boy. But Livingstone was out; it was his day off. I would have to do something with the remains myself. A further large shot of Gordon's fine remorse remover quickly eased my woe, and a half hour later I went back to retrieve the body.

But the body was nowhere to be seen.

I looked around the pen.

Nothing.

Then a slight movement in the darkest corner of the run caught my attention. There he was, fully recovered and on his feet, worrying away at some invisible fleas he had suddenly discovered among his far back feathers. He was preening himself as if he had won the World Heavyweight title, but he was carefully avoiding any eye

196

contact with me. The preen complete, he trotted off to another distant corner, stopping only for a second or two to seduce an innocent hen pecking away nearby.

I waved him a friendly greeting.

'Well done Sir,' I said. 'You <u>are</u> a mighty champion, and I salute you. Can we be friends?'

I do not know how highly scientists rate the intelligence of domestic fowls, but I can tell you they are not stupid. My Uitkyk Cock, who I honoured by naming him Lord Nelson, for his blind eye and brilliant strategic vision, adopted me after that singular encounter. He made me president of our small republic, and whenever I entered his domain he would fearlessly fall in beside me, and strut along with me step for step, inspecting the troops.

Leaving Home
Mike Rook

The die was cast at the turn of the century when Zimbabwe started its long and painful slide into perdition, sinking slowly at first but soon plummeting into the abyss at the speed of light. The cost of living was on its way to the stars, jobs were being lost as fast as the value of the dollar was dropping, and abject poverty inevitably followed. Sadly, not the slightest sign of concern was expressed by the government.

The mortal blows that led to this economic implosion were the wilful and sudden destruction of the country's agriculture, combined with large unbudgeted cash hand-outs to troublesome war veterans. The value of the Zimbabwe dollar dropped by something like 30 per cent overnight.

One of the many drastic side-effects of Zimbabwe's chaotic land reform programme was the closure of the vast majority of companies that were servicing and supplying the agricultural industry. The company I headed became one of the first of many to suffer serious collateral damage. As a result the jobs and livelihoods of me and my colleagues were prematurely demolished. I had been involved in the production of farming publications since 1979.

Although it was a shocking revelation, when the axe fell I was not too concerned as I had received many offers of freelance work. This kept me busy for a while. I stayed optimistic, as I believed the madness would stop, sooner rather than later.

Personally I was in good enough financial shape: good pension provision, nice house and late model car all fully paid up.

I was looking forward to a relaxed, happy, secure and trouble free retirement in the country that I loved and called home: in the land where my children were born and had grown up.

As 2002 gave way to 2003 Zimbabwe's malaise gathered pace, almost as fast as the quality of life faded. It was exceedingly tough for almost everyone, except of course for the ruling party sycophants shouting praises at the President.

For those like me with a child or children at school, budgeting for massively inflated fees and the basic necessities of life had become mission impossible. The words 'disposable income' disappeared from our vocabulary.

Particularly frightening aspects of the tottering economy were the unaffordability and shortages of essential drugs, and the massively escalating charges of medical attention. Health care had become beyond the pockets of most Zimbabweans. Average life expectancy was falling fast. Aids fatalities in particular were increasing due to sufferers being unable to pay for, or find the medication. Even those fortunate enough to source medicine through a non-governmental organisation, were losers, because the lack of a proper diet totally negated the medication's usefulness.

Month on month inflation was creeping up to shocking and unbelievable figures. It began to dawn on stressed Zimbabweans that much worse was yet to come. There were no queues for mealie meal, meat or for fuel; nothing was available. The only long queues were at the passport offices up and down the country. Every day thousands of Zimbabweans were desperately trying to get out and seek sanctuary elsewhere. South Africa and the United Kingdom were choice destinations. It wasn't long before both countries were forced to implement a closed door policy, effectively imprisoning hungry desperate jobless Zimbabweans in their own country. Nevertheless it is estimated that over three million Zimbabweans left and are still living away from their homeland.

My ability to ride out the storm started to crack in June 2005. Income from my informal freelance work had shrunk, and with the formal unemployment figure running at over eighty per cent I found myself at the end of a cul-de-sac. To keep my son at school and meet living expenses I first sold my car and then my house. The idea behind these two crucial and momentous decisions was to increase my capital, and thus my income from the additional interest. What I needed so desperately was more time. My son was in Form four and writing his Cambridge ordinary level examinations and I was trying to build up my media business. There was only the two of us to worry about. In September of

2006 we moved into a two bedroomed flat in the Avenues. We went in on a sixth months' lease at a monthly rent of thirty million Zimbabwe dollars.

Frightening as that thirty million figure was, more dramatic inflationary increases were to come.

For the two of us, the end came suddenly and brutally in January 2007, just four weeks before the flat lease was set to expire. It was in the form of a letter from the estate agent giving us notice. The owner was selling the property.

Enquiries confirmed that if alternative accommodation was available the rent would be pitched at approximately twice the amount we'd been paying, around sixty million per month. I didn't even ask about the deposit.

As carefully and as many times as I did my sums I found expenditure always ahead of income. It was at last time up, and time to leave. The one and only silver lining in a black cloud of despair was that my son had completed his public examinations and his school year.

A few hours before heading for the airport my son and I packed what clothes we could into two suitcases.

I thought that Harare airport seemed strangely quiet and subdued, almost in a state of mourning that seemed to mirror the feeling throughout the nation. We had struggled to lift our cases onto the baggage scales. They were most definitely overweight – not surprisingly since we were trying to take as much clothing as we could pack. Even though we had millions of Zimbabwe dollars to pay for excess baggage it was not enough.

We would have needed tens more millions, and so there was no option except to dig into our suitcases and remove items of clothing from an already depleted wardrobe. It was a dreadful setback.

Soon we found ourselves wandering through the duty free shop. We were almost alone except for one or two fellow travellers grabbing bottles of quality liquor. The local supermarkets and bottle stores had not stocked such imported luxuries for years. With paper worth a few hundred thousand Zimbabwe dollars left over we left the booze alone and decided to buy chocolate. We had no foreign money and no idea therefore when we might eat again after our arrival. My son also bought himself a lucky charm bracelet to remind him of home.

At the airport's inner sanctum we sat patiently waiting for the announcement to board. I wondered how many others booked onto the flight were also saying a final goodbye to their motherland. If not leaving for good themselves, many were going to visit loved ones already exiled and to look around with an eye to emigration.

Juice to feed the aeroplane's engines had finally been located and one by one and two by two passengers entered the connecting tube snaking from the terminal exit to the aircraft door. The flight from Harare left very late but eventually we were on our way.

I am not ashamed to say that as the big jet lifted off Zimbabwean soil and started its climb over the outskirts of Harare there were tears rolling down my cheeks. My son's tears had come much earlier before leaving the public area of the airport. Unlike me, he was born in Zimbabwe and had never before left his native Africa.

Next morning, March 18, was cold with an ominous dark sky overhead as we descended into Gatwick Airport. I peered out the cabin window only to see thick greyish clouds scudding by. Only minutes before landing was there visual contact with the runway.

After taxiing to the terminal we left our cosy and comfortable transportation, but not before my son and I had exchanged handshakes and smiles with the cabin crew. Air Zimbabwe was to us the final connection with home. When that last umbilical cord was severed, I had a distinct feeling of foreboding. The chilly wind blowing through the airport terminal dampened our spirits even further. We were, like millions of other Zimbabweans, forced out of our beloved country in order to get a life and to find a new future. We had no idea of what lay ahead. We had left behind lots of worthless money, a land without employment opportunities: a land with nothing to buy and little to eat. Yet it was home and we were indescribably sad to be saying goodbye.

Standing on a moving walkway overlooking the airport apron I stared in awe at the dozens of parked aircraft from airlines I never knew existed. The two of us, father and son, made our way towards the baggage collection area. Trolley at the ready, we collected our worldly belongings, and then passed through immigration and customs without incident. We truly had nothing to declare.

Suddenly we were in the public domain, alone and penniless in the midst of the madding crowd. The information desk and the Travel Care staff at Gatwick's south terminal have seen it many times before. They've witnessed victims of civil wars and misrule from Africa, Asia, Eastern Europe, and from all corners of the earth. My son and I were just two more in an endless stream of innocent victims.

I knew we were in for a rough ride ahead, but for my son it all seemed an amazing adventure. Having said that, I salute his courage, tenacity, optimism; and most of all his invaluable support.

With him by my side, I knew that failure was not an option.

205

Made in the USA
Columbia, SC
04 December 2023

27723683R00129